ROADSIDE NATURE TOURS

{ *through the* }

OKANAGAN

. . . . .

ROADSIDE NATURE TOURS

{ *through the* }

OKANAGAN

A GUIDE TO BRITISH COLUMBIA'S
WINE COUNTRY

RICHARD CANNINGS

GREYSTONE BOOKS

D&M PUBLISHERS INC.

Vancouver / Toronto / Berkeley

Greystone Books
A division of D&M Publishers Inc.
2323 Quebec Street, Suite 201
Vancouver BC Canada V5T 4S7
www.greystonebooks.com

Library and Archives Canada Cataloguing in Publication
Cannings, Richard J. (Richard James)
Roadside nature tours through the Okanagan : a guide to British
Columbia's wine country / Richard Cannings.

Includes index.

ISBN 978-1-55365-288-5

1. Natural history—British Columbia—Okanagan Valley (Region)—Guidebooks.
2. Okanagan Valley (B.C. : Region)—Guidebooks. I. Title.

FC3845.O4A3 2009   917.11'5045   C2008-907350-9

Editing by Kathy Sinclair
Cover and text design by Naomi MacDougall·
Cover photograph by Graham Osborne
Photos by photographers credited
Printed and bound in Canada by Friesens
Printed on acid-free paper that is forest friendly
(100% post-consumer recycled paper) and has been processed chlorine free
Distributed in the U.S. by Publishers Group West

We gratefully acknowledge the financial support of the Canada Council for the Arts,
the British Columbia Arts Council, the Province of British Columbia through
the·Book Publishing Tax Credit, and the Government of Canada through the Book
Publishing Industry Development Program (BPIDP) for our publishing activities.

⊰ CONTENTS ⊱

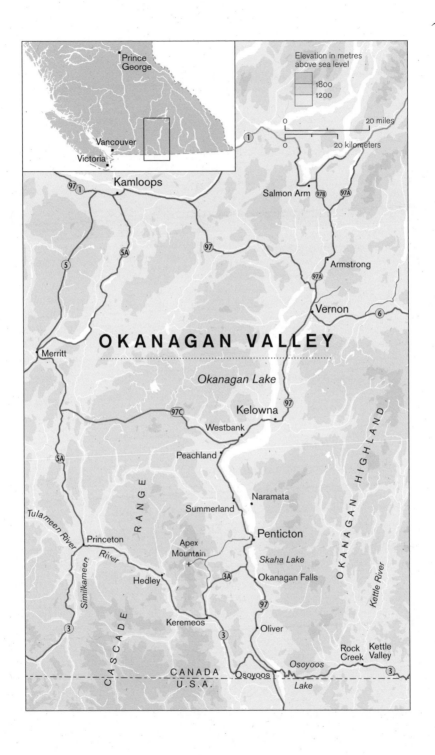

Prince
George

Vancouver

Victoria

Elevation in metres
above sea level

1800
1200

0   20 miles

0   20 kilometers

1

97 1   Kamloops   Salmon Arm 97B   97A

97   Armstrong

5A   97A

5   Vernon   6

Merritt

OKANAGAN VALLEY

Okanagan Lake

97C   Kelowna   97

Westbank

Peachland

Naramata

Summerland

R A N G E

Tulameen River

Princeton   *River*

Penticton

Apex
Mountain

Skaha Lake

3A   Okanagan Falls

Similkameen

Hedley

O K A N A G A N   H I G H L A N D

Kettle River

97

Keremeos

3   Oliver

Rock   Kettle
Creek   Valley

C A S C A D E

CANADA
U.S.A.

Osoyoos

3

Osoyoos
Lake

(WINE & WILDLIFE)

TUCKED INTO THE EASTERN flanks of the Cascade Mountains is a narrow valley unlike any other in Canada—the Okanagan. This small watershed is only 30 to 60 kilometres wide and extends 170 kilometres from Osoyoos in the south to Armstrong in the north. The Okanagan has a dry climate but is filled with a series of large lakes that moderate the hot days of summer and the Arctic airflows of winter. The lakes and small streams of the valley also provide water that has transformed most of the desert grasslands in the valley bottom into lush orchards and vineyards. And packed into this valley are some of the rarest and most fascinating plants and animals in the country.

When I was young, my hometown, Penticton, used to advertise itself as the "City of Peaches and Beaches." In fact, a concession stand in the shape of a giant peach still sits on the shore of Okanagan Lake. In those days visitors came to the Okanagan Valley for just that combination—a week or two with the family to lie on glorious natural sand under the hot sun, followed by a quick stop at the fruit stands on the way home to Vancouver or Calgary to stock up on cherries, apricots, peaches, and apples.

Although I grew up on an apple orchard and spent perhaps too many of my boyhood summer days on the sunny lakeshore, I always knew the Okanagan was much more than peaches and beaches. Our family often hosted keen birders and young biologists who came to enjoy the valley's other riches—an incredible diversity of plants and animals, many of which were difficult to find anywhere else in Canada. I quickly developed a strong sense of pride about how special this place was and have carried that feeling ever since.

After living in the urban excitement of Vancouver for more than twenty years, I was drawn back to the Okanagan in 1995 by my deep love for the region. Things had changed, of course— twice as many people lived in Penticton than when I last lived there, and five times as many in Kelowna. But I also got the feeling that more local residents shared my feelings about the natural Okanagan and that more tourists were coming just to see spring wildflowers and listen to birdsong, to climb the rugged cliffs along Skaha Lake, and to cycle along the historic and spectacular Kettle Valley Rail Trail. Shortly after I settled in, I got a phone call from the local chamber of commerce suggesting that we form a group to organize an annual nature festival, an event that would have been unthinkable when I was a child.

I also noticed that the agriculture industry was changing rapidly. Apple, pear, and apricot orchards were being converted to vineyards, driven by the discovery that the local soils and climate were ideal for growing high-quality grapes for fine wines. When I was a teenager, people noted Okanagan wines only for their low prices and matching quality, but my new neighbours in Naramata produced wines that were winning awards around the world. More and more people were coming to the valley specifically for its wines; I even led a couple of weekend "wine and wildlife" tours for visitors from Vancouver to take advantage of this change in focus for tourism. My participants agreed that an exciting morning of birding followed by a delightful lunch on a patio with a glass of chilled Ehrenfelser was hard to beat on a warm spring day.

In the thirteen years since I moved back to the Okanagan, this shift in tourism has continued to the point where nature- and wine-loving visitors make up a significant part of the annual tourist population, although sun-lovers still crowd the beaches in July and August.

To paraphrase James Thurber, "I don't know much about wine, but I know what I like." I do, however, know a bit about natural history, and I hope that this book will allow visitors who come for wine or wildlife—or even some hot sunshine—to explore some of the Okanagan's roads with fresh eyes for its natural treasury and to come away with a richer sense of what makes this valley one of the best places on Earth.

The Natural Okanagan

Although the Okanagan's reputation for fine weather may be enough to bring visitors from the rain-soaked coast of British Columbia or blizzard-bound Alberta, one natural feature of the valley stands out as an obvious attraction: its diversity. Few places in Canada—or even North America—can boast its combinations of desert sands and deep lakes, towering rock cliffs and rich benchlands, and cold mountain forests and hot grasslands. Freezing winds carve back the needles on stunted firs at tree line, while only a few kilometres away a rattlesnake slides around yellow cactus flowers, hunting for pocket mice. Cattail marshes line river oxbows only a few metres from sagebrush that sends roots deep into dry soils in a constant quest for water.

This wide array of habitats is not only refreshing for the hiker or biker but a real boon to wildlife. The presence of permanent water in such an arid landscape greatly boosts the numbers and varieties of animals able to live in the area. And the statistics are impressive. About 200 species of birds nest in the Okanagan Valley, more than anywhere else in Canada. In fact, few places in North America could boast such an impressive list in such a small area—arctic birds on the mountaintops, boreal forest birds in the spruce, coastal forest birds in the cedars, and southwestern desert birds in the sagebrush. No wonder birders come from all over the continent to the Okanagan to add to their life lists. Every May teams of birders from all over British Columbia participate in the Okanagan Big Day Challenge, competing to see how many kinds of birds they can see in one crazy day in the Okanagan. I was on the team that set the long-standing record of 174 species.

And it's not just birds, of course. Fourteen species of bats live in the Okanagan, more than anywhere in Canada, including the spectacular spotted bat, which looks like a little flying skunk with oversize pink ears. The valley is also the British Columbia hot spot for reptiles and amphibians, featuring spadefoot toads, tiger salamanders, rubber boas, and, at least formerly, pygmy short-horned lizards. One little pond near Penticton is home to almost half the dragonfly species of British Columbia. Most other invertebrate species are not well surveyed, but the presence of northern scorpions, Jerusalem crickets, and black widow spiders certainly adds spice to a prowl through the grasslands.

4

Another quality of the natural environment that draws visitors to the Okanagan is rarity. Many of the Okanagan's plants and animals are found nowhere else in Canada or at least are very difficult to find elsewhere. The canyon wren is found from southern Mexico to the rocky cliffs just south of Kelowna, and the sage thrasher from Arizona to the White Lake Basin west of Okanagan Falls; the Lyall's mariposa lily grows only on the east slope of the Cascades from central Washington north to Osoyoos; and the list goes on.

In Canada, most of the plants and animals unique to the Okanagan are associated with habitats at low elevations—the dry grasslands on the valley benches and moist woodlands and marshes along the lakes and streams. These habitats, in turn, have been the prime landscapes settled and irrevocably altered by human settlement in the past century. The Okanagan has the biggest concentration of species at risk in the country, and almost all of these species are endangered because of that combination of rarity in Canada and habitat loss. Some estimates suggest that 80 per cent of riparian habitats—the birch woodlands along the old channels of the Okanagan River and the marshes at the head of each lake—and 50 to 70 per cent of grasslands have been lost to agriculture and urban development.

The Building of the Okanagan Valley

Two hundred million years ago, there was no Okanagan Valley. Indeed, very little land stood where British Columbia is today— just the shallow waters of the continental shelf of western North America. Then, starting about 180 million years ago, a series of continental collisions occurred. Large island masses, perhaps similar to Japan or the Philippines, slid into the west coast of North

America, carried by drifting continental plates. These landmasses pushed up and overrode the sedimentary rocks on the shelf, creating much of the land area of British Columbia.

The collisions continued off and on until about 60 million years ago, when the dynamics of the colliding plates changed and the tremendous pressure that had built the mountains of British Columbia largely ceased. As the eastward pressure eased, the great piled mass of southern British Columbia slumped back to the west, allowing huge cracks to appear in the land. These cracks—called relaxation faults—are some of the large valleys of British Columbia we know today—including the Rocky Mountain Trench, the Kitimat Trench, and the Okanagan Valley.

As the Okanagan Valley opened, the sedimentary rocks laid down on the old continental shelf of North America rose to the surface after being deeply buried for more than 100 million years. They had been greatly changed—melted and recrystallized into hard metamorphic rocks such as gneiss. The high rock cliffs of the south Okanagan, including the massive wall of McIntyre Bluff north of Oliver, are almost all part of this group. The rifting process that opened the Okanagan Valley was accompanied by a great deal of volcanic activity. Many of the smaller mountains in the valley—for instance, Munson Mountain in Penticton, Giant's Head in Summerland, Mount Boucherie near Westbank, and Knox, Dilworth, and Layer Cake mountains in Kelowna—are all made of volcanic rock from this period.

For the next 50 million years or so, nothing truly dramatic happened to the Okanagan landscape. Vast outpourings of lava blanketed the Columbia Basin to the south and the Chilcotin Plateau to the northwest; some of these flowed onto the Thompson Plateau at the north end of the Okanagan, cooling into columnar basalts. The mountains slowly eroded, as mountains always do, creating rounded plateaus on either side of the valley.

Then the ice came. About 2 million years ago, the Earth's climate cooled as the Pleistocene Epoch began. More snow fell each winter, and the summer melt decreased. Snow accumulated rapidly in the mountains of British Columbia, forming glaciers that flowed out of the Coast, Columbia, and Rocky mountains and filled the valleys. The glacier flowing south through the Okanagan Valley grew until it overtopped the plateau on either side and joined other river glaciers to form a vast ice sheet almost 2 kilometres thick. Covering all but the highest peaks in the province, this ice sheet flowed inexorably west to the sea and south over the Okanagan and other valleys to melt on the Columbia Plateau in what is now Washington State. The Pleistocene wasn't constantly cold; it contained a half-dozen or more long periods within it when the world was warmer than it is today. The glaciers shrank and advanced with each climatic cycle; the latest major advance began about 30,000 years ago and reached its maximum extent about 15,000 years ago. Shortly after this peak, the climate warmed again, and the ice quickly melted back and was more or less gone by 12,000 years ago.

The ice sheet melted from the top down as well as from its leading edges, so the first areas free of ice were the mountaintops and plateaus, and the last remnants of the Pleistocene were huge masses of ice in the valley bottoms. Old rivers flowed again as the ice melted, but they often found their ancient paths blocked by valley glaciers or altered forever by the deep scouring action of the ice. In the south Okanagan, a large, lingering mass of ice created a big plug at the narrowest point of the valley—the rock cliffs south of Vaseux Lake. The Okanagan River backed up to form a large

7

lake, called Glacial Lake Penticton, that stretched 170 kilometres north to Enderby. Like all glacial lakes, it was a milky blue colour from the large amount of fine glacial flour it carried, silt scoured off bedrock by thousands of years of glacial flow.

The glacial flour settled to the bottom of the lake each year, forming a deep layer of pale material called glaciolacustrine silt. The river flowed north out of Lake Penticton into the Thompson and Fraser systems until the plug at McIntyre Bluff melted so that the Okanagan could flow once again into the Columbia. The shaping of the Okanagan Valley was complete—the glaciers had rounded off the plateau hills and cut the valley broad and deep. Like all fiord lakes, Okanagan Lake is very deep—about 232 metres at the deepest point. Meltwater streams filled other parts of the valley with huge amounts of sand and gravel carried down from the scoured plateaus. The glaciolacustrine silts form conspicuous white cliffs along the shores of Okanagan and Skaha Lakes but are noticeably absent south of McIntyre Bluff, the site of the plug that formed Lake Penticton.

Ecosystems

To make sense of the tremendous natural diversity of the Okanagan, it helps to divide the region into ecosystems. At the simplest level, there are four of these: the narrow ribbons of dry grasslands on the benchlands on either side of the valley bottom; the coniferous forests that stretch to the mountaintops; the islands of alpine tundra that cap the highest peaks; and the lakes, rivers, marshes, and other water-rich habitats.

The desert grasslands really characterize the Okanagan and set it apart from other lake-filled valleys in Canada. At first glance, these grasslands might appear to be rather monotonous and less

8

diverse than the forests above, especially on a hot August afternoon when the dry soil crunches underfoot and the songbirds are silent. A closer inspection, however, quickly reveals a beauty and richness equal to any rain forest. The bunchgrasses here differ from grasses of the Canadian prairies in several ways, but primarily in that they actively grow only in spring, when soil moisture is adequate. By July the hillsides are parched, and the grasses, their nutrients stored in a large mass of fibrous roots, turn gold. The grasses wait out the summer drought and winter chill then green up again in spring. Many prairie grasses, adapted to moister summers, do not form distinct bunches but instead grow more evenly across the ground almost like a turf.

If you look at the grass itself, you will see that there are several kinds of bunchgrass common to the Okanagan, each indicating subtle differences in rainfall, temperature, and soil structure. Many valley-bottom grasslands in the south Okanagan are dominated by red three-awn grass, with its thick clumps of fine leaf blades and a three-parted seed head that looks exactly like the centre of a Mercedes-Benz logo. At slightly higher elevations, the southern grasslands are dominated by the tall tufts of bluebunch wheatgrass, with its seeds arranged on vertical stems like tiny beads on a string. This is the archetypal bunchgrass that fed the cattle industry, which in turn shaped the history of the West. Drier locations are often covered by needle-and-thread grass, whose seeds are essentially miniature spears that easily attach themselves to passing cattle and humans. Healthy upper-elevation grasslands in the southern valley, such as those on Anarchist Mountain east of Osoyoos and in the rolling hills around Vernon in the northern valley, are dominated by fescues, bunchgrasses with more feathery seed heads.

9

But perhaps the commonest grass of all in the Okanagan is a newcomer: cheatgrass. A native of southern Europe, its barbed seeds are shorter and more insidious than those of the needle-and-thread, filling socks and shoes with a mass of painful points. Cheatgrass is an annual plant, its seeds germinating in fall then flowering the following spring. The small plants don't form bunches; their predilection for overgrazed sites has allowed cheatgrass to blanket entire landscapes across the Intermountain West.

Are these grasslands really a pocket desert, as the area around Osoyoos Lake is often called? The combination of sandy soils, cacti, rattlesnakes, and scorpions certainly fits the public perception of a desert. The annual rainfall is about the same as that of southern Arizona, and no one would dispute that the area around Tucson, with its saguaro cacti, is a desert. But many ecologists say that the presence of perennial grasses in the Okanagan Valley—the bunchgrasses mentioned above—indicates that these grasslands are a steppe. More particularly, they would call it a shrub steppe, because the grasses often grow in association with woody plants such as antelope brush and sagebrush.

Like the different grasses, each of these shrubs adds its own character to the ecosystem. Antelope brush is found in the southern half of the Okanagan Valley; its dark, gangly limbs are often associated with red three-awn, and together the two form one of the most endangered plant communities in the country. The sandy soils are dotted with clumps of brittle prickly pear cacti and serenaded by the songs of the lark sparrow. The present endangerment of this community is due at least in part to its increasing value as prime grape-growing land.

Sagebrush covers the dry hills of the southern valley as well, primarily on the west side. It seems to be found on more loamy soils than antelope brush and is often associated with bluebunch wheat-grass. Several species of birds and other animals are closely tied to sagebrush to the point where they are rarely found more than a stone's throw from the aromatic grey shrubs. Sage thrashers nest throughout the dry western valleys of North America, north to the White Lake Basin just west of Okanagan Falls. Another songbird with a close attachment to sagebrush is the Brewer's sparrow, which reaches the northern limit of its range just west of Penticton.

Throughout the grasslands there are scattered ponderosa pines—big, veteran trees with glowing brick-red bark and long green needles. As you climb off the benches and onto the surrounding hills, these trees become more common and quickly coalesce into park-like woodlands. This change from grassland to forest marks the lower tree line. Ponderosa pines are the tree species in this region most tolerant to drought and high summer temperatures. They are the classic conifer of the dry valleys and mountains of the West, evoking images of cowboys riding through sunlit glades. Like sagebrush, ponderosa pine woodlands host a suite of species found in no other habitat. The pygmy nuthatch is perhaps the bird most tightly bound to ponderosa pines; this small bird roams the forests in flocks that comb the furrowed bark and large cones for insects and other food items. A more enigmatic ponderosa pine specialist is the white-headed woodpecker, a strikingly patterned bird that specializes in eating pine seeds through the winter; in Canada this woodpecker is found only in the south Okanagan Valley.

Ponderosa pine forests have changed dramatically in the last century. Indigenous people burned these forests on a rotating schedule for thousands of years, setting fires on cool autumn days to clear out small trees and shrubs that encroached on the grassland understory. The large pines have a very thick bark, allowing them to survive the ground fires and maintain the open, park-like structure—large, scattered trees with a grassy understory—so characteristic of these dry forests. When the West was settled by Europeans in the late 1800s and early 1900s, this method of forest management was abruptly stopped, replaced by logging of the large trees and active suppression of fires. Throughout much of the West—and the Okanagan is no exception—this has resulted in dense stands of young ponderosa pines, each fighting for scarce water resources and shading the light-starved plants on the forest floor.

As you climb higher on the hillsides, average temperatures drop and average precipitation increases, and with these differences comes a similar change in tree species. Douglas-fir gradually replaces ponderosa pine; then it, in turn, is replaced by western larch, Engelmann spruce, and subalpine fir. The plateaus on either side of the valley are covered largely by dense growths of lodgepole pine. Ecologists call lodgepole pine a seral species—a tree that pioneers open ground after a fire or logging, then gives way after a century or two to spruce and fir. In recent decades much of the lodgepole pine in British Columbia has been decimated by mountain pine beetles, and as a result, the forest industry has targeted it with massive clearcuts.

A few rounded peaks rise above the upper tree line in the Okanagan Valley. The forest opens up to green meadows with scattered whitebark pine; higher still, the trees are reduced to wind-pruned clumps of twisted branches, and flowers bloom from cushions tucked out of the wind behind lichen-covered rocks. This is alpine tundra, where summers are too short and too cool to allow tree germination.

12

In a valley with little rainfall, watery habitats play a disproportionate role in shaping the natural landscape. Not only do the large lakes provide year-round water, they also moderate daily temperatures, particularly in winter, allowing species that would otherwise have to move out or hibernate to stay active. And the lush growth around marshes, lakeshores, and river oxbows provides a rich food source used by almost every wildlife species in the valley at one time or another. The broad-leaved trees along the shores—birches, cottonwoods, and aspens—are highly attractive to many birds and mammals. They grow quickly and are commonly attacked by various heart rots, producing hollowed trunks that provide snug homes for woodpeckers, owls, squirrels, raccoons, and many other species.

Like the grasslands, these rich, moist environments have been disproportionately affected by human settlement—lakeshores are naturally the most favoured sites for housing and resort developments. Perhaps the project that affected these habitats the most was the channelization of the Okanagan River in the 1950s. This project completely altered the water flow in the system, flushing spring runoff through the valley as quickly as possible. Salmon runs dwindled, affected by both the drastic changes in local channels and the construction of eleven dams downstream on the Columbia River. The wet meadows and birch woodlands along the old meandering river channel were then converted to agriculture or housing, and as the seasonal flow disappeared, the few that remained became shadows of their former selves.

Climate

The Okanagan Valley has a reputation for being a hot, dry place; the sandy benchland of the Osoyoos area is often called Canada's

13

pocket desert. The valley does indeed lie in the rain shadow of the Cascade and Coast mountains, and so moist Pacific air is wrung dry as it rises over these ranges on its eastward track in from the ocean. This maritime flow is one of three airstreams that dominate the local climate; the other two are the warm continental flow from the Great Basin to the south and the frigid air that creeps down from the Arctic in winter.

One of the most important factors that affect the Okanagan climate is the presence of large lakes through most of the valley. These lakes significantly moderate the climate throughout the year, warming the valley in winter and cooling it in summer.

The south Okanagan receives about 30 centimetres of precipitation per year. This is certainly less than in most parts of the province, but it is not the driest area—sites such as Ashcroft and Keremeos, tucked into deep valleys in the eastern flank of the Cascade and Coast ranges, often get less than 25 centimetres. Rainfall increases gradually as you go northward in the valley and then rather sharply near the north end; Kelowna gets 31.5 centimetres and Armstrong 44.8 centimetres of precipitation each year.

Spring comes early to the Okanagan in comparison with other inland areas in western Canada. As the days lengthen in February, the track of the Arctic airstream shifts eastward, allowing warm Pacific air to flood in from the coast. The snow quickly melts in the valley bottom, and the first spring flowers—sagebrush buttercups and yellowbells—brighten the golden grasslands. By the end of February, the first spring migrant birds have returned from the south—tree and violet-green swallows take in the early midge hatches over the river, and western meadowlarks sing again. By late March the apricots are blooming white throughout the southern valley, followed in April by the pink peach, white cherry, creamy pear, and white and pink apple blossoms. Wild currants are blooming too, and the first hummingbirds come back to take advantage of the new nectar.

The spring air warms rapidly, and on hot days in late May, you can often see children swimming in the lakes—adults usually wait until July. Most of the birds have returned by the end of May; pink bitterroot blossoms appear as if by magic out of the hot, dry soil, and cottonwood fluff drifts through the air like snow in a summer snowstorm. Although precipitation is relatively even throughout the year in the Okanagan, June is the wettest month. Warm rains melt the deep snowpack in the mountains, and all the creeks swell, sending frigid, silty water into the lakes. Sometime in early July, a strong high-pressure ridge builds to the west, deflecting the moist Pacific airstream north into the Yukon, and the dry and hot days of a classic Okanagan summer settle in, fuelled in part by oven-like air flowing north out of the Great Basin Desert. Young birds leave their nests, and the laneways of the valley fill with scuttling groups of tiny quail.

The Pacific airstream reestablishes itself in late August, bringing fall showers back to the Okanagan. Songbirds such as warblers and flycatchers stream south, heading for winter quarters in Central America. Shorter days and a lower sun bring lower temperatures, and by early October the mean temperature on the mountaintops falls below freezing. The larches on the eastern slopes of the valley turn brilliant gold, and the cottonwoods along the creeks soon follow with a similar show of colour. The frost line drops steadily; the first snow flurries bring temporary washes of white to the valley bottom in November. As small lakes in northern and central Canada freeze, rafts of coots, ducks, and other waterfowl appear on the lakes of the Okanagan.

15

The real cold is yet to come, however. Sometime in December or early January, the first stream of Arctic air slips through passes in the Rockies and slides into southern British Columbia. Overnight lows drop below –10°C, and vineyards spring into action to harvest the frozen grapes for icewine. Snowfalls now blanket the ground for weeks on end. Snow depths in the south Okanagan rarely exceed 15 centimetres but are regularly over 30 centimetres in Kelowna and even deeper in Vernon. Armstrong receives a total of 135 centimetres of snow each year, compared with only 60 centimetres in the southern parts of the valley. Snowfall also increases with elevation, of course; some subalpine areas can get over 500 centimetres of snow, much to the delight of local skiers.

Early History

As the glaciers receded from the Okanagan, animals and plants recolonized the rock and gravel left behind. The climate warmed quickly, and the landscape was rapidly transformed into a mosaic of forests and grasslands. Among the new arrivals were people who came to hunt the game, harvest the plants, and take the salmon from the reestablished river.

The Native people of the Okanagan call themselves Syilx and are part of the Salish language group. The name Okanagan, first recorded by Lewis and Clark as Otchenaukane in 1805, has an obscure history. It is usually translated as "going towards the head," but exactly how this word relates to the valley is unclear. One explanation suggests that it refers to people travelling up the Okanagan River to the head of the lake near Vernon, and another refers to seeing the top of sacred Mount Chopaka from near Osoyoos. There were four major settlements in the valley in the late 1800s: one at the north end of Osoyoos Lake at Nk'Mip; one on the flats between

Okanagan and Skaha Lakes at Penticton; one at the north end of Okanagan Lake at Nkamaplix; and one at Spallumcheen near Armstrong. These settlements were used throughout the winter, when the people lived in *kekulis* (circular structures built partly underground for warmth) and ate the foods that they had harvested and stored throughout the warmer months.

In spring, family groups would leave these settlements to travel throughout the Okanagan territory to a complex array of traditional food-harvesting sites, including spring fishing grounds in the Similkameen, bitterroot (*speetlum* in the Okanagan language) patches on the southern grasslands, and saskatoon berry (*siya*) patches throughout the valley. In late summer, families would camp in high mountain meadows to pick huckleberries, while others gathered in larger groups at salmon concentrations in the south Okanagan and at Kettle Falls to the southeast. Hunter families would harvest deer and other game in the fall, but as the days shortened and snow began to fall on the mountains, most families would return to the permanent settlements for the winter. Apparently enough resources could be found around Penticton to warrant year-round residence there, since its name means "people always there."

The earliest Europeans to visit the Okanagan were fur traders; Scotsman David Stuart is reputed to be the first of these to see the valley, in 1811. The Okanagan quickly became an important trade route; furs were packed south from the northern forests of British Columbia to Fort Kamloops, then down the Hudson's Bay Company Brigade Trail through the Okanagan Valley to the Columbia River at Fort Okanogan, and from there to the Pacific at Fort Vancouver and Fort Astoria. David Douglas, the famous botanist who first identified the Douglas-fir, travelled north along this route in the spring of 1833. The fur trade waned sharply in the middle of the 1800s when silk replaced beaver felt as the latest style in European hat fashion. The Brigade Trail was also replaced by a more western route in 1846, when the establishment of the forty-ninth parallel as the border between the United States and British North America forced Kamloops traders to travel west of the Okanagan to the mouth of the Fraser River.

British Columbia joined Canada in 1871, and one of the first results of that union was the creation of Indian reserves throughout the new province. Reserve boundaries were drawn over a period of years, starting in the late 1870s, and then often redrawn as ranchers and developers lobbied the government for choicer parts of the valley. The reserves changed the lifestyle of the Native population completely: summer food harvests were gradually disrupted, and traditional habitat management tactics, such as prescribed burns, were essentially outlawed immediately.

Cattle, Cherries, and Chardonnay

One of the earliest impacts of European colonization in the Okanagan Valley was the arrival of the cow. In the 1860s large ranching operations were set up to provide beef for the miners who had flocked to British Columbia during the Cariboo Gold Rush and other, similar strikes. By 1864 there were about 14,000 cows in the valley, and that number rose to 26,000 by 1890—about 20 cows for every human. These cattle were grazed year-round on the arid grassland benches in the valley bottom and drastically altered that habitat. The grass species west of the Rocky Mountains evolved without the herds of bison that continually grazed the prairie grasses, so they were not adapted to constant grazing pressure. Much of the low-elevation grasslands changed from thigh-high bunchgrass to dusty stubble.

By 1900 most of the large cattle ranches were being broken up for development. Townsites sprang up throughout the valley, and the dominant agricultural landscape changed from ranches to orchards. Early orchards were irrigated by a system of flumes and canals that diverted water from local creeks to the upper parts of the orchards. Water was directed through the trees by a series of smaller ditches. In the early 1900s, ground crops such as tomatoes, cantaloupes, and watermelons were extensively planted between trees, but as the trees matured into full production, these crops were phased out. Many early orchardists also kept cattle and chickens for extra income, growing alfalfa between the trees for forage.

Agricultural development continued through the first half of the 1900s, so that by 1950, almost all the private land in the valley bottom was either urban or orchard. Agriculture dominated the local economy; forestry activities in the early 1900s were concentrated on providing timber for local development, including the construction of flumes and apple boxes.

A few vineyards were planted as early as the 1920s, and Calona Wines began production in the late 1930s. The wine industry blossomed in the 1960s and 1970s but generally produced inexpensive and decidedly inferior wines. In 1984 Canada and the United States signed a free trade agreement that allowed duty-free importation of American grapes for processing in the few large Okanagan wineries. Many predicted that this would spell the end of the Okanagan vineyards, and large acreages of vines were pulled up, particularly along Black Sage Road in Oliver. However, a few small estate wineries were having remarkable success with

19

European vinifera grapes, and the number of these small operations began to grow quickly. As of 2008, more than 100 wineries in the Okanagan and Similkameen valleys use grapes from more than 3,000 hectares of vineyards. Winemakers have found that the long, hot summers at the south end of the valley are ideal for Bordeaux varietals such as Cabernet Sauvignon, Cabernet Franc, and Merlot, while vineyards in the cooler, northern sections of the valley are well situated for German wines such as Gewürztraminer, Riesling, and Siegerrebe.

Now the orchardists struggle most with cheap imported fruit, and grape growing provides better monetary returns than almost every tree fruit except cherries. As apple, apricot, pear, and peach prices remain in the doldrums, every winter now brings new scenes of orchards being pulled up, burned, and replaced with the more lucrative vines.

More than just the agricultural scene is changing in the Okanagan. The valley has always been a favoured destination for people, luring them with its mild climate, warm waters, and diverse wildlife. Each year new residents arrive, pushing housing developments upslope into pine forests and filling marshlands with condos. But unlike their predecessors, most of these new colonists are choosing the Okanagan for its natural beauty, and hopefully, they will promote the intelligent regional planning necessary to preserve this richness.

This book explores that natural legacy along a series of highways and byways throughout the valley. Some of the subjects of discussion can be easily seen from a moving car—the black snags of a forest fire, hillsides covered in spring flowers, an osprey landing on its pole-top nest with a big carp. To see other fascinating denizens of the valley requires occasional stops and walks through the grasslands and forests. If the weather permits, drive along with your windows open so that you can smell the soft aromas of sagebrush and pine and hear the meadowlarks sing. Some of the routes described are short drives that can be completed in less than an hour, whereas a few are more ambitious and could be all-day adventures. ·

(ROAD TRIPS)

SOUTH OKANAGAN

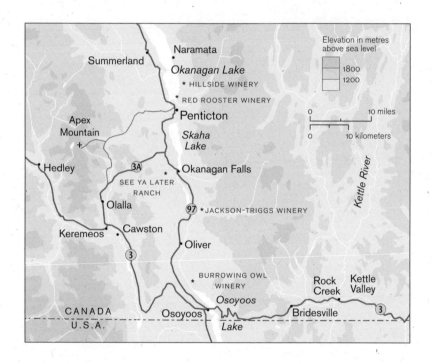

Summerland

Naramata

Okanagan Lake

★ HILLSIDE WINERY

★ RED ROOSTER WINERY

Penticton

Apex Mountain
+

Skaha Lake

Hedley

3A

Okanagan Falls

SEE YA LATER RANCH

Olalla

97 ★ JACKSON-TRIGGS WINERY

Keremeos

Cawston

3

Oliver

BURROWING OWL WINERY
★

Rock Creek

Kettle Valley

CANADA
U.S.A.

Osoyoos

Osoyoos Lake

Bridesville

3

Elevation in metres
above sea level

1800
1200

0   10 miles

0   10 kilometers

Kettle River

ANARCHIST MOUNTAIN TO ROCK CREEK

48 km, all paved highway

This route will take you from Osoyoos to Rock Creek,
where you can then retrace your steps, continue east along
Highway 3, or travel to Kelowna on Highway 33.

START: Junction of Highways 3 and 97 in Osoyoos;
travel east on Highway 3.

HIGHWAY 3, THE CROWSNEST HIGHWAY, takes a dramatic route east out of Osoyoos, climbing the steep western flank of Anarchist Mountain. Earlier trails wound back and forth across the international boundary that marks the southern edge of Osoyoos, following a much gentler path east of Oroville, Washington. But in the 1920s, highway engineers were forced to stay north of the border and to build the highway up the face of Anarchist Mountain in a series of spectacular switchbacks. This route starts at the bridge over the narrows of Osoyoos Lake.

A convenient pull-off on the east side of the bridge allows you to take in the view north and south. Looking in either direction you might find it hard to imagine the landscape before motels, condos, apricots, and grapes. Osoyoos Lake was once surrounded by sandy grasslands dotted with dark antelope brush and scattered ponderosa pines. Large marshes sat at the north and south ends of the lake and on the south sides of its peninsulas. Native people gathered here to catch the salmon that migrated north through the narrows in September; evidence of long-term encampments and important burial grounds is nearby.

27

To the south you can see the long peninsula of Haynes Point, which sticks out into Osoyoos Lake from the west, almost reaching the eastern shore. Only 30 metres wide and a kilometre long, the point ends in a long sand spit that turns into a shallow ford across the remaining 400 metres of the lake. It was here that Native people and early white visitors crossed the lake on foot or on horseback. The Okanagan name for this place is Sw'iws, meaning "low water allowing people to cross." The narrows where the highway crosses, though a shorter distance, was deeper and more difficult to ford. The Native name for that site is Souyous, meaning "narrow waterway where land almost meets," the origin of the name Osoyoos.

From October through April, Osoyoos Lake is an important migratory stop and wintering ground for waterfowl. Loons, grebes, ducks, geese, and swans all congregate on the lake, and the narrows where the bridge is located is a favourite spot for many of them. The lake often freezes—especially the shallower south end—in December and January, but the slight current in the narrows usually keeps the water open there. Osoyoos Lake is also important for fish stocks. The largest sockeye salmon run in the Columbia River system spawns in the Okanagan River just north of Oliver, and the juvenile salmon spend a year in Osoyoos Lake before migrating down to the Pacific. A handful of chinook salmon also spawn in that area, but the numbers are so reduced that the stock is considered threatened in Canada. The lake's warm waters make it difficult for salmon to survive in midsummer, and its position at the downstream end of a heavily populated watershed means that it also carries a relatively heavy load of nutrients and other pollutants.

Just as you leave the strip of motels on the east side of Osoyoos, you will see signs for the Nk'Mip Desert Cultural Centre. Only a kilometre off the highway, on 45th Street, this award-winning centre run by the Osoyoos Indian Band has displays and programs interpreting Native and natural history, as well as nature trails through the desert grasslands to the north. Of particular interest is the centre's rattlesnake research program—many of the resident snakes have been individually marked, and some even carry tiny radio transmitters so that biologists can study their movements.

Leaving Osoyoos, the highway makes the first big switchback through the orchards and begins to climb Anarchist Mountain's steep slopes. You pass a relatively new vineyard just below the highway, and about 3 kilometres from the big corner you cross tiny Haynes Creek, named after J.C. Haynes, the first government agent in the Osoyoos area. Small creeks such as this are very important to wildlife in this dry environment. In the heat of late summer, many birds move into the leafy shade of the Douglas maples, birch, and aspen for the rich supply of food they need to ready themselves for their southward migration in late August.

Just past the creek, you make another sharp turn back to the left and another to the right; then, on the third corner, you'll see a viewpoint pull-off on the right (this is available only to uphill travellers; those coming downhill have a pull-off a little higher up). Be sure to stop here if you can—the scene is spectacular. The boundary between green agricultural lands and the surrounding native grasslands is striking—a telling commentary on how irrigation can irrevocably change a landscape. You are just a kilometre from the United States at this point—the border is along the far side of the small reservoir lake immediately south of (and well below) the viewpoint. Looking to the northwest over the western shores of the lake, you can see the long ridge of Mount Kobau. Mount Kobau was once chosen to be the site of a major optical telescope, and a wide road was built to its summit (section 2). Although government austerity programs ended that plan, the dry, clear Okanagan air has resulted in several private observatories being set up on Anarchist Mountain just above this viewpoint.

Above the viewpoint, the highway leaves the steep mountain slopes to follow Haynes Creek up a small, lush valley filled with birch and ponderosa pine. At the next big switchback corner, the highway touches the site of a large forest fire that burned the slopes of Anarchist Mountain in July 2003. This fire, which was started by sparks that came from the defective brakes of a vehicle travelling along the highway just above Osoyoos, burned 1,230 hectares and two homes; it was the first large fire in the Okanagan in a summer that would become the worst forest fire season in local history.

The highway continues to climb through second-growth ponderosa pine woodlands and past a rest stop, then levels out into a wide expanse of open grasslands. These grasslands are quite different from those in the valley bottom. Shrubs such as sagebrush and antelope brush are rare or absent, and the dominant grass species tend to be fescues instead of wheatgrass and three-awn. The grasslands here are similar to the valley-bottom grasslands around Vernon, at the north end of the Okanagan Valley, and have a fauna to match. Columbia ground squirrels, called "gophers" by many, are common here, and Anarchist Mountain is one of the better places in British Columbia to see their major predator, the badger. These big, stripe-faced members of the weasel family are endangered in the province, having suffered decades of habitat loss and direct persecution—ranchers did not appreciate their predilection for digging large burrows on cattle land. One of the main threats

‹ Williamson's sapsucker: male (left), female (right)

focus › **Larches and Sapsuckers**

Remnant patches of moister forest here are dominated by western larch, one of the most magnificent trees in the West. This fast-growing conifer is, like all of its larch cousins, a deciduous tree. Its fine needles turn brilliant gold in October and fall to the ground, then regrow as bright green new foliage in the spring. The western larch is a favourite tree for all sorts of wildlife, since the older specimens are often hollow-centred, providing nest sites for woodpeckers, owls, squirrels, and other animals. One of the real specialties in this habitat is the Williamson's sapsucker, a small, handsome woodpecker that prefers the larch above all for its nest sites. This bird drills straight lines of tiny holes on Douglas-firs and larches to harvest the sap that emerges. This energy source helps fuel the sapsucker's searches for its main prey: carpenter ants. The ants, in turn, maintain herds of aphids that they milk for their sugary sap. Most of the old larch forests on Anarchist Mountain have been cleared for farm fields or simply logged for timber, but a few pairs of sapsuckers cling to the blocks of woodland that remain. Their numbers have dwindled to the point that they are considered endangered in Canada.

31

to their existence now is the dangerous life they lead following—and crossing—major highways such as this.

In the summer, watch for Swainson's hawks circling overhead or perched on power poles. These broad-tailed, broad-winged hawks look for mice or large insects such as grasshoppers. In the autumn they make a very lengthy migration to the Pampas of Argentina, travelling in large flocks through the isthmus of Panama. In winter, you may see rough-legged hawks that have migrated south from breeding grounds in the Arctic tundra to Anarchist Mountain to catch mice in the grasslands of southern Canada and the northern United States.

As you pass the junction with Sidley Mountain Road, you can easily see the international boundary again, still about a kilometre south of the highway. This marks the former site of Sidley, a small townsite founded by Richard G. Sidley in 1889. Some say that Anarchist Mountain got its name because of Sidley's attitude towards the finer points of law in his own private border town.

About 27 kilometres from Osoyoos and 1,233 metres above sea level (almost a vertical kilometre above Osoyoos), the highway reaches Anarchist Summit and enters the Kettle River drainage, another of the major tributaries of the Columbia. Copses of aspens nestle into hollows in the grassy hills north of the highway. To the south, on the north-facing slopes of Baker Creek, dense green forests of Douglas-fir are a marked contrast. You quickly slip by the tiny community of Bridesville, named after an early settler, David McBride. About 7 kilometres east of Bridesville, the highway crosses Rock Creek as it flows through a narrow canyon 93 metres below the bridge deck. After passing Johnstone Creek Provincial Park, the highway descends steeply—yes, one more switchback—to

32

the town of Rock Creek on the banks of the Kettle River. From here you can pause at the local café or pub then retrace your steps to Osoyoos, continue eastward on Highway 3 to Grand Forks and beyond, or turn north up Highway 33 (section 17) and make a long loop to Kelowna. · · · · · · · · · · · · · · · · ·

2

RICHTER PASS, MOUNT KOBAU, AND THE SIMILKAMEEN

46 km, paved highway with two optional, gravel-road side trips

*This route takes you from Osoyoos to Keremeos, where you can
continue west on Highway 3, travel to Penticton on Highway 3A,
or travel to Oliver via Blind Creek Road (gravel).*

START: Junction of Highways 3 and 97,
Osoyoos; turn west on Highway 3.

HIGHWAY 3 CLIMBS west out of Osoyoos on a long, relatively straight
hill, radically different than its twisted course east of town covered in the previous section. Only a half-kilometre from the
Highway 97 junction, the road swings northwest as you pass over
the remains of the old South Okanagan Land Project canal that
brought irrigation water to orchards on the west side of the valley
for many years. Built in 1919, the canal runs from the Okanagan
River north of Oliver south to Osoyoos; this southern section was
abandoned when it became easier to pump water from Osoyoos
Lake than to use gravity-fed water from the canal.

The highway travels along a flat bench with an airstrip on the
northeast side of the road; this bench is a remnant terrace from
glacial times, when a huge block of stagnant ice filled the valley.
Meltwaters from the surrounding plateaus carried sand and gravel
into the valley, depositing them in flats around the ice. When the
big ice block melted, it left a hollow that was filled by the Okanagan River to become Osoyoos Lake.

The viewpoint near the top of the first long hill (about 5 kilometres from Highway 97) is well worth a stop. From this vantage

34

you can easily appreciate the effect that irrigation has had on the lower grasslands. Across Osoyoos Lake are the large acreages of grapes planted by Vincor, with the last remaining substantial area of antelope brush grassland visible between the northern section of vineyards and the Nk'Mip development east of the Osoyoos townsite.

Violet-green swallows chatter overhead, flying in and out of nest sites in clefts in the rocky cliffs above the highway. Ravens and magpies are often seen here as they loaf above the Osoyoos Landfill, occasionally joined by a golden eagle. On the flat directly below you is the site of the Osoyoos Desert Centre, accessible from 146th Avenue off Highway 97. From May through early October, the centre provides guided tours of the desert grasslands—their ecology, conservation, and restoration—along a 1.5-kilometre boardwalk (www.desert.org).

The road levels off a bit at the top of the long hill, travelling through rolling grasslands dominated by big sagebrush. You soon pass Spotted Lake, a striking alkaline pond filled with mysterious salt circles, on the southwest side of the road. These circles are made of epsom salts—mostly magnesium and sodium sulphates, with small amounts of sodium carbonate and calcium sulphate. The rings are thought to be formed through crystallization processes driven by the alternate flooding and drying of the lake. You'll also find a small pull-off with an information kiosk halfway along the lake. Local Native peoples—who call the lake Kliluk—consider it sacred; the Okanagan Nation owns the lake, and access is not permitted.

Just past Spotted Lake, you pass a few sloughs that were once rich marshes full of waterfowl and other animals in summer, but they are now mostly dry, because their spring meltwater sources

35

> *bitterroot flower*

side trip › **Mount Kobau**

At Richter Pass, a good gravel road goes off to the northwest to the top of Mount Kobau. This is well worth a side trip on a sunny day, as the peak (1,863 metres) provides one of the best viewpoints in the south Okanagan. The road, just over 19 kilometres long, winds its way up through a diverse mosaic of grasslands and Douglas-fir forests. Interestingly, the sagebrush grasslands extend all the way to the top of the mountain, making Mount Kobau one of the few mountains in Canada where grasslands link the upper and lower tree lines. Spring and summer are delayed by altitude, so flowers that bloom in May in the valley bottom (for instance, bitterroot) can be found blooming in July on top of Mount Kobau. The curious mix of sagebrush and subalpine fir at the peak results in an equally interesting combination of animals—lowland birds such as Brewer's sparrows sing alongside high-mountain specialists such as hermit thrushes. The short walk to the old forestry lookout from the parking area gives you spectacular views of both the Okanagan and Similkameen valleys. Much of the mountain is protected from development, though large sections are private land.

Mount Kobau—with its combination of high elevation, easy access, and clear, dark skies—was selected as the site of a major optical telescope in the 1960s, and the wide road was built to provide access for the large trucks needed to transport equipment up the mountain. Plans changed and the telescope was eventually built in Chile, but amateur astronomers still gather on the mountain every August for a "star party."

go to domestic and agricultural uses. At the top of the next hill you reach Richter Pass—at 682 metres elevation, a pass so low you aren't even at the lower tree line, let alone near the alpine tree line. Summers are too hot and dry here for trees to germinate successfully; at the upper tree line atop local mountains, summers are simply too short for trees to grow.

Continuing southwest over Richter Pass, you descend a long hill through the Elkink Ranch. This was once the Richter Ranch, one of the big spreads in the Okanagan-Similkameen in the early 1900s. Watch for chukar, a species of partridge, along the roadside. These striking birds, with bright red legs and bills and sandy-coloured plumage set off by a bold black necklace, are native to southern Europe and the Middle East. The steep, rocky hillsides around Richter Pass and other parts of the south Okanagan are very similar to the rugged, dry habitats in the chukar's homeland, and the bird has prospered since being introduced to this part of Canada in the 1950s. On spring mornings the males can often be heard giving their low, cackling *chukar-chukar* calls from prominent rocks.

Another interesting bird often seen along this route is the Lewis's woodpecker, one of the strangest woodpeckers in North America. These birds excavate nest holes like other woodpeckers, preferring the big, old ponderosa pines that stand like sentinels in the midst of the sagebrush. But the Lewis's are otherwise very unwoodpecker-like. They look and act like small crows much of the time, with glossy black plumage and steady, rowing flight— totally different from the bounding flight typical of the woodpecker family. At close range they are strikingly beautiful, with bright pink breasts, elegant grey collars, and deep wine-red faces. They have two methods of foraging, neither of them the usual getting-bugs-out-of-dead-trees tactic used by their cousins. In summer they spend hours in high, circling flights like giant swallows, hawking large insects out of the air. In late summer and fall, they turn their attentions to the abundant supply of berries and fruit available; native species such as saskatoons and chokecherries are suitable, but in the modern era, the birds' favourites are cherries and grapes. In September they migrate to the oak woodlands and almond orchards of California to feed on nuts, returning again in early May as the bugs start to fly.

The highway's southwestward course brings it back towards the international boundary, and it must make a broad northward turn to stay in Canada. At the southernmost part of this turn is the junction for the road that makes the 3-kilometre trip to the United States border at Chopaka Customs and on to Nighthawk, Washington. This road is popular with birders and botanists, since it provides access to some of the best sagebrush habitat in Canada (public land on the west side of the road only). It was also the location of the last sighting of white-tailed jackrabbits in British Columbia. These large hares are still common on the Canadian prairies—even in suburban Edmonton and Calgary—but the British Columbia population proved too sensitive to hunting pressure and habitat loss to survive and was extirpated in the 1980s. The last confirmed sighting was in the summer of 1981, when I saw three of these big hares just north of the border.

As the highway turns north, it drops into the steep-walled valley of the Similkameen River. The river winds through a floodplain dotted with ponderosa pine/cottonwood woodlands and lush pastures; it flows south across the border and eventually joins the Okanagan River at the south end of Osoyoos Lake. At

focus ＞ **Sage Thrasher**

If you are lucky, you might spot one of Canada's rarest birds on the fence lines south of Richter Pass—the sage thrasher. Thrashers are relatives of mockingbirds and catbirds, which are found in shrubby habitats across North America; sage thrashers are restricted rather tightly to the dry sagebrush steppes of the West. Slightly smaller than the American robin, they look nondescript with their sage-grey plumage and lightly streaked breasts, but the males have a lovely, long, warbling song that drifts over the sage early on summer mornings. In Canada they are found only in the Richter Pass area and the White Lake Basin (section 4) west of Okanagan Falls, although pairs sometimes take up temporary residence in similar habitats of southern Alberta and Saskatchewan.

the confluence of the two rivers, the Similkameen is about three times the size of the Okanagan.

Although similar to the Okanagan in climate, the Similkameen Valley is closer to and more firmly in the rain shadow of the Cascade Mountains. Storms streaming west from the Pacific lose almost all their moisture as they climb over the cold peaks, producing the strong but dry winds that so commonly race through this valley. Annual precipitation at Keremeos is only about 20 centimetres, compared with 30 at Osoyoos and Penticton.

The hay fields of the Similkameen are home to long-billed curlews and bobolinks, two birds rare in British Columbia. Curlews are the largest of the North American sandpipers and are characterized by long, curved bills that they use to pick up grassland insects on their breeding grounds and probe for intertidal worms on their mudflat wintering grounds in the subtropics.

Bobolinks are small songbirds related to blackbirds and meadowlarks; the females look like brown sparrows, but the males have a most unusual plumage. Most birds—indeed, most animals—have a basic colour pattern: they are dark on top to match the ground when viewed from above and light underneath to match the sky when seen from below. Male bobolinks are the opposite—jet-black below and white and cream above. This pattern sets them off against both backgrounds as they fly over the meadows, singing their bubbling songs to attract the attention of females. Populations of both curlews and bobolinks are threatened across the continent by the loss of natural grasslands.

The village of Cawston was the site of a Hudson's Bay Company outpost starting in 1860, when Fort Okanogan (near Brewster, Washington, where the Okanagan River meets the Columbia) was abandoned to the United States and the company needed another site to winter livestock north of the border. This post—called Shimilkameen in most records—was short-lived, closing in 1872 as trade across the new border slowed.

The Similkameen Valley shares many rare species with the Okanagan, but it has at least one to itself: the Mormon metalmark. This small, orange-and-black butterfly can be found in only a few sites in the province, all in the Similkameen Valley around Keremeos. It has a curious habitat preference: gravelly slopes sparsely vegetated with snow buckwheat and common rabbitbrush. The adult butterflies feed on the nectar of the rabbitbrush's golden flowers in late summer, and the females lay their eggs on the soft grey leaves of the buckwheat, the only plant the larval caterpillars will eat. So few of these butterflies remain in the province that the population is listed as endangered.

Just north of Cawston, the highway crosses the tiny channel of Keremeos Creek as it winds across the bottomlands of the Similkameen River. This creek gives the town of Keremeos its name, since the Native word means "creek that cuts through the flats." From Keremeos, you can continue west on Highway 3 towards Vancouver or return via Highway 3A to Penticton. An alternate route is the gravel Old Fairview Road, which is reached via Upper Bench and Lowe roads; this route snakes up through sagebrush and aspen then into Douglas-fir before reaching a pass at about 1,075 metres elevation. It then descends to the Fairview area of west Oliver. · · · · · · · · · · · · · · · · · ·

3

MCKINNEY ROAD TO MOUNT BALDY

40 km, 12 on pavement, the rest on a good gravel road

This route takes you east out of Oliver on a gradual climb to the plateau, eventually reaching Mount Baldy, one of the few points in the Okanagan above tree line.

START: 350th Avenue and Highway 97, Oliver.

FROM HIGHWAY 97, turn east at the stoplight in Oliver—350th Avenue—and continue across the Okanagan River channel bridge. Immediately after the bridge, keep right and follow 362nd Avenue up past the hospital and on to the Osoyoos Indian Reserve. You are on McKinney Road, named after Camp McKinney, a mining site high on the plateau to the east that was important in the late 1800s. Black Sage Road (section 5) exits right (south) off McKinney Road at this point, but keep going straight east for this route. You will be travelling through the Osoyoos Indian Reservation for the next 10 kilometres; please don't trespass off the road along this stretch.

The road crosses the South Okanagan Land Project canal, which comes out of the Okanagan River at McIntyre Bluff about 8 kilometres north of here and terminates just south of McKinney Road. Built in 1919, the canal is still used today as a water source by many of the orchards and vineyards along its length. After the canal, the road winds into a small valley formed by the waters of Wolfcub Creek. Sandy bluffs on the left (north) side of the road are honeycombed with the nesting burrows of bank swallows.

42

These birds nest in large colonies, digging burrows about a metre deep into sandy surfaces. The males dig the new burrows with their bills, feet, and wings; the burrows protect well against potential nest predators such as hawks and snakes. Being insectivorous, the swallows migrate south in the fall, spending the winter in the warmer climes of South America and returning north in April.

The road climbs out of the creek valley and on to a large, flat terrace. This is Manuel's Flats, one of the terraces built during the final stages of the glacial period, when sand and gravel were carried out of the mountains and into the valley. The flats built up against the huge glacier that melted in place in the valley bottom. Today they are covered by bunchgrass and sagebrush; they can look desolate on a hot summer afternoon or cold winter day but are alive with song and activity early on a spring morning. Meadowlarks sing from all sides, Brewer's sparrows belt out their buzzy, canary-like songs, and long-billed curlews give their mournful, whistled calls. Other animals are more secretive, especially the many insects restricted to these dry grasslands. One of them is the ground mantis, Canada's only native mantis. These insects look like small sage twigs; their cryptic coloration makes them very difficult to find. The females are wingless, so they never fly and give away their position as the larger praying mantises—introduced from Europe—often do.

At the end of the flats, the road climbs gradually through the lower tree line into ponderosa pine woodlands. This is the preferred habitat of the western bluebird, so watch for the flashes of indigo as the birds fly to nest boxes on the fence posts and trees near the road. Near the kilometre 7 point (logging truck drivers use the kilometre signs on the trees to radio their position to their

43

focus ▸ **Western Rattlesnake**

Few animals are as widely feared and as poorly understood as the rattlesnake. These reptiles are fairly common but rarely seen in the dry grasslands of the British Columbia Interior and probably reach their highest Canadian population density in the lowlands of the Okanagan Valley from Oliver south to Osoyoos. The western rattlesnake has a line of brownish ovals down its back, somewhat different from the dark brown, distinctly rectangular patches on the back of the gopher snake. If you see the tail, the interlocking scales on the end that form the rattle are distinctive, especially if they are buzzing like a maraca.

Rattlesnakes are largely nocturnal, especially on warm summer nights, tracking their small mammal prey with special heat-sensitive pits near their nostrils. They have long front fangs that fold back when the mouth is closed but open and lock in place to deliver a dose of poison when the snake attacks. Rattlesnakes rarely bite humans; they usually slither quietly away without even so much as a warning rattle. The venom is rarely fatal to humans; its main effect is to start the digestion process, breaking down muscle, arteries, and veins and making the bitten leg or arm blacken and swell. If you encounter a rattlesnake on a trail and it stands its ground, simply back away and detour around it.

Rattlesnakes are long-lived reptiles, and each female gives birth to about five live young only every third year. Because of this slow reproductive capacity, rattlesnake populations are very sensitive to losses from willful killing and roadkill. Be careful when driving back roads in the south Okanagan at night; drive slowly so that you can avoid snakes that are crossing or basking on the warm road surface.

coworkers), the road crosses Wolfcub Creek. Although a relatively small stream, Wolfcub Creek is important to a host of wildlife species, since it provides water throughout the summer in this arid environment. At about kilometre 10, you leave the Indian reserve and enter a mix of public and private lands. A stop at the first cattle guard past the kilometre 10 sign will give you a good taste—or at least smell—of ponderosa pine woodland. Stick your nose into the orange bark and enjoy the aroma of fresh vanilla—the chemical in the bark is the same one used to make artificial vanilla.

I stopped at this point in May 1986 and heard a grey flycatcher calling—*chelep chelep, chelep sweep!*—the first time this species had been found breeding in Canada. These quintessentially drab birds were traditionally known only from the Great Basin deserts of the American West, but in the late 1960s they began moving north from central Oregon, reaching southern Washington in the early 1970s. They have spread a short distance in the last twenty years and are now found throughout the south Okanagan Valley in open pine forests.

After you pass kilometre 11, watch out on the left for a larger-than-life-sized wooden woodpecker nailed to a tree. This marks "Woodie's Landing," a famous spot in the birding lore of British Columbia where a family of white-headed woodpeckers foraged regularly from 2001 through 2004. The rare birds were attracted to this actual spot not by the pines—though ponderosa pine is an essential part of their habitat in the northern half of their range—but by the concentration of mullein in the clearing at the roadside. These spear-like plants are considered an introduced weed, but their seed heads are very attractive to small woodpeckers and chickadees.

The road meanders up through small patches of older ponderosa pine forest, then into a forest dominated by young Douglas-fir. At kilometre 17 it drops into the Baldy Creek valley, which has a nice stand of spruce mixed with western larch. This remnant patch of old-growth forest is home to a number of interesting birds, including a pair of barred owls that nest in one of the large veteran trees.

As you climb out of the Baldy Creek valley, you enter public forest lands, and the dominant landscape is one of clearcuts regenerating to thick, young pine forests. These areas provide a good lesson in forest succession. When they were cut in the 1980s, they closely mimicked the grasslands in the valley bottom, and an array of grassland birds—mountain bluebirds, vesper sparrows, western meadowlark—moved in. Within a few years, the willows, alders, and young aspen had taken over in places, giving moose and elk a good source of winter browse and shrub-nesting birds such as dusky flycatchers a place to breed. The dense stands of lodgepole pine that are there now don't attract much in the way of birds or mammals, except for widespread generalists such as dark-eyed juncos and yellow-rumped warblers. It will be two hundred years before a climax forest of Engelmann spruce and subalpine fir will become established, boosting the diversity of the region with a long list of species tied to that ecosystem. Unfortunately, forest harvest policies will likely short-circuit the natural progression, returning the site to a thick, young pine forest before the spruce can mature.

At about kilometre 22, you pass a series of wetlands called Coteay Meadows. These are typical plateau sedge marshes, often enhanced by the work of beavers or human engineers with the

47

aim of retaining spring meltwaters throughout the year. You can often see moose feeding in the shallow water, and common yellowthroats, northern waterthrushes, and Lincoln's sparrows call from the sedges. Before the forests around the ponds were cut, a small colony of great blue herons nested there.

The road goes over a small ridge at kilometre 27, marked by a microwave tower on the south side of the road. The tower is surrounded by a remnant patch of veteran western larch and Engelmann spruce—a great place to look for rarer woodpeckers such as Williamson's sapsucker and the American three-toed woodpecker.

Coming up from Highway 3 just past kilometre 33, you meet Mount Baldy Road; turn left and you'll reach the ski village in about 6 kilometres. You are now in pure subalpine forests dominated by subalpine fir and Engelmann spruce. Winter wrens bubble in the thickets, and fox sparrows sing their beautiful whistled songs from the dense brush. Mount Baldy, of course, gets its name from the treeless tundra at its peak; the Native name is *Pak-kum-kin*, meaning "white top." A trail to the top of the mountain makes for a pleasant hike on a hot summer day—watch for alpine specialties such as American pipit and white-tailed ptarmigan if you get above tree line.

You can return to Oliver the way you came or take a longer loop back to Highway 3 near Rock Creek (section 1). · · · · · ·

4

FAIRVIEW–WHITE LAKE ROAD

28 km, all paved

This is one of the classic back-road routes in the Okanagan, linking Oliver to Penticton with a relatively quiet paved road.

START: Highway 97 traffic light in Oliver at 350th Avenue.

TURN WEST OFF the highway onto 350th Avenue and proceed across a bench of orchards. The road then climbs through a small, winding gully filled with water birch and chokecherry. Watch for a sign of a small colony of bank swallows—a cutbank filled with holes—on the left at the bottom of the hill. On summer mornings, you can also listen along the birch draw for the loud whistles of yellow-breasted chats. These large songbirds are considered endangered in British Columbia, since their deciduous thicket habitat has been largely converted to housing and orchards over the years. The males' songs are a startling variety of loud whistles (like someone whistling for a lost dog), rattles, and squawks.

After a couple of tight corners, the road reaches a broad slope, the alluvial fan of Reed Creek, which drains the mountainside to the west then goes to ground in its own gravel. This slope was the site of Fairview, a once-thriving mining town that simply vanished a few years after the gold supply dried up. My grandfather worked here in the winter of 1907–08, cutting firewood for the steam-driven stamp mill that crushed the gold ore. When my father was born in Penticton in 1914, his birth was registered in Fairview, the main government office in the south Okanagan at that time.

49

By 1920 all the buildings of Fairview had either burned or been moved down the hill to the new community of Oliver.

The gravel soils of Fairview were not considered good for orchards, so the land has largely reverted to its natural state— bunchgrasses and antelope brush. Near the top of the slope, turn right (north) at Fairview–White Lake Road. This road travels through open ponderosa pine woodlands, then hillsides covered in grass and shrubs such as saskatoon and mock orange. This was all thick ponderosa pine forest until 1970, when a major forest fire burned 4,000 hectares west of Oliver. The slow reestablish-ment of ponderosa pine here is testament to the hot, dry summers that inhibit tree germination. Very few trees have reseeded in the burn area, despite a series of moist summers in the mid-1980s. As summers become longer and hotter over the next century in the Okanagan Valley and fires become more common, more ponde-rosa pine forests will be converted to grasslands.

Another outcome of long, hot summers—and increasing devel-opment—is the lowering of local water tables. The small pond on the west side of the road about 2 kilometres north of the Fairview junction is often much larger—sometimes extending for several hundred metres—but lately it is usually only a small circle of water.

After passing a short series of small rural holdings, the road begins to follow a tiny stream that drains Burnell (Sawmill) Lake in the hills to the west. The birches along the creek are a good place to look for hummingbirds—the males often perch atop dead branches to watch for passing females. The two common species in this habitat are black-chinned hummingbirds (males have a solid black throat and green flanks) and calliope hummingbirds (males have a streaky spray of magenta feathers on the throat).

A green gate on the west side of the road marks the access track to the Susie Mine, a shaft dug to extract gold. Now abandoned and blocked with a grate, the shaft is well-known among local biologists as an important roost site for bats. The Okanagan Valley has the highest bat diversity in Canada, with fourteen species flying through the summer night skies. Just past the Susie Mine, you'll pass the University of British Columbia Geology Camp, a collection of rustic buildings on the west side of the road. Each year, students spend a few weeks in May at a field school, sited here because of the tremendous diversity of geological formations in the south Okanagan.

North of the geology camp, the road follows Victoria Creek, a slightly bigger brook that drains another pair of lakes in the hills to the west, Madden and Ripley. Secrest Road branches off to the east, providing a shortcut back to Oliver via Highway 97. If you take that route in April, watch for a spectacular showing of yellow balsamroot flowers òn the sandy bench.

Keeping left on the Fairview–White Lake Road, you pass through a remnant grove of old ponderosa pines spared by the 1970 fire. This habitat is favoured by western bluebirds, attracted by the nest boxes unobtrusively affixed to the pine trunks. The road then follows the west edge of a large flat covered by high grasses. This area, known as Meyers Flat, is formed from the deposits of four small creeks that filled this basin with sand and gravel; most of the water flow here is below the ground. The public land around Meyers Flat is part of the White Lake Grasslands Protected Area, set aside by the provincial government to protect the rare and diverse natural heritage in the hills between Okanagan Falls and White Lake.

52

focus › **Big Sagebrush**

Sagebrush is one of the iconic plants of the West. Its soft grey foliage and distinctive aroma define many of the valleys and high plains from New Mexico to central British Columbia, where it reaches its northern limit along the Fraser River west of Williams Lake. Even though they are usually only a metre or so high, the plants provide shade and cover for all of the wildlife species found in the grasslands they inhabit, and many of those species are so closely tied to sagebrush that they are rarely found away from it. Three birds are even named after it—the sage grouse, the sage thrasher, and the sage sparrow; there are also the sagebrush buttercup, the sagebrush mariposa lily, and the sagebrush vole.

Sagebrush is superficially similar to two other common grassland shrubs in the Okanagan; its three-toothed leaves distinguish it from the common rabbitbrush, which has narrow, linear leaves, and the soft, grey look to its foliage separates it from the larger, ganglier antelope brush. If you have any doubt, just gently crush some leaves in your fingers; the sharp smell of sage should be immediately obvious.

Like cedar bark, sagebrush bark is fibrous, aromatic, and easily stripped off the larger stems. It likely has insect repellent properties similar to those of cedar as well. Sage thrashers strip the bark off the stems to line their sage-twig nests. The bark was also used by local Native people to weave fabric for clothing.

Although sagebrush is still widespread, about 70 per cent of its former range in western North America has been converted to agriculture or burned and replaced by introduced grasses such as crested wheatgrass and cheatgrass. Many of the animals reliant on it are considered species of concern in both Canada and the United States.

The north end of Meyers Flat is taken up by the rural community of Willowbrook. As you pass it on the west, you come to the junction of Green Lake Road on the right. This is an interesting route to Okanagan Falls (section 7). For now, keep going straight north, and note the alfalfa fields on the west side of the road. The road enters a small draw, with open ponderosa pine forests on the east side and dense Douglas-fir forests on the west.

After winding through the upper part of the draw, the road reemerges into the main valley, with a small creek, Park Rill, hugging the west side of the road. This route was part of the famous Hudson's Bay Company Brigade Trail, along which fur traders carried goods between Fort Kamloops to the north and Fort Okanogan, on the Columbia River, to the south. Many of these traders were French–Canadians, and Park Rill got its name from the French *parc*, meaning "corral"—after an encampment along the stream west of White Lake. The road then leaves Park Rill and winds up a hill, eventually emerging into the large White Lake Basin, a natural bowl of sagebrush and grass about 2 kilometres across. This is one of the most well-known natural areas in the valley and the site of intensive conservation work over the past few decades.

The cliffs along the east side of the basin are composed almost entirely of volcanic rock. About 55 million years ago, when the Okanagan Valley was forming, this area was a very active volcanic site, and the White Lake Basin was filled with layers of lava and sediments about 3,000 metres thick. The basin has no outlet; all spring meltwaters find their way into White Lake, an alkaline pond in the southeast quadrant of the bowl. There they gradually evaporate in the increasing heat of the spring days, and by summer—sometimes even as early as late April or May—there is nothing left but an expanse of greyish-white salt.

For a brief period in spring, the lake is a frenzy of life. The water quickly fills with brine shrimp, the small crustaceans popularly known as "sea monkeys." These animals mature rapidly, mate, and produce eggs that can withstand the prolonged dry period each year. The shrimp are fed upon by Wilson's phalaropes, attractive little sandpipers that spin in the water to stir the animals up, then pick them up with long, pointed bills. Phalaropes are unusual in the bird world in that the females are larger and more brightly coloured than the males. The females display to attract the males, mate with them, then leave them—a true reversal of roles. The males then incubate the eggs and raise the young by themselves. Flocks of ducks use the lake as a migration stopover on their way to breeding grounds in central British Columbia, the Yukon, and Alaska. In wet years, a few pairs of ducks or grebes may even stop to nest at White Lake, but the lake usually empties quickly as the waters disappear into the hot summer air.

The spring waters also bring in two amphibians of the dry grasslands. Great Basin spadefoot toads gather along the shores of White Lake in late April, the males croaking loudly to call in females. Spadefoot eggs hatch quickly, and the tadpoles develop within a month in a race to become air-breathing adults before the water dries up. Tiger salamanders also come here to mate and lay eggs, but the lake produces adult salamanders only in years when the waters are deep and the spring is cool and wet, so that the lake remains full well into summer. Both these species spend their adult lives in the dry grasslands of the basin, hunting insects and other small prey by night. They also share the habit of burrowing deep beneath the ground to escape the scorching heat of summer and the frosts of winter. They are both considered species at risk because of habitat loss in the British Columbia grasslands.

55

A green metal gate at the southern entrance to the basin points the way to a dirt track that leads down to the lake and beyond. An interpretive sign explains the conservation efforts that are underway around White Lake; the Nature Trust of British Columbia owns a ranch on the west side of the basin and controls grazing on the rest of it. The organization's goal is to maintain grazing on the land in such a way that it does not degrade the biodiversity of the area, a common problem when there are too many cows and too little grass.

The big attraction at White Lake for naturalists is its healthy cover of big sagebrush. While sagebrush is also found in abundance north of the Okanagan in the Thompson and Fraser valleys, White Lake is the northern limit for a number of animals that are dependent on this plant for survival. A few pairs of sage thrashers nest here in most years, and you can usually hear good numbers of Brewer's sparrows giving their long, trilling songs. The common birds in the grasslands are western meadowlarks, which fill the spring air with loud, musical song, and the less conspicuous vesper sparrows, flashing white outer tail feathers as they fly away through the shrubs. If you walk through the sagebrush, you can usually see the tunnelling runways of montane voles cut through thicker areas of grass. These greyish, short-tailed mice are related to lemmings and have similar population cycles; when vole populations are up, the mouse-hunting birds stop to nest, and you might be lucky enough to see a northern harrier coursing over the grass or a pair of short-eared owls hunting in the late evening.

The road comes to a T-junction as it reaches the north side of the basin. A left turn will take you to Twin Lakes and then out to Highway 3A, where you could continue on to Keremeos and

Vancouver. We will turn right to return to Highway 97 just south of Penticton.

At the northeast end of the basin you can't help but notice a huge array of poles and wire and several large parabolic antennas pointed at the sky. This is the Dominion Radio Astrophysical Observatory, a National Research Council project that probes the most distant parts of the universe. It was sited here because the natural bowl at White Lake shields the observatory from most radio interference from the outside world. The pole-and-wire array was used to map various sources of long-wave radio emissions in the Milky Way as well as more distant galaxies. These long waves can only penetrate the Earth's atmosphere during periods of very low sunspot activity, so they were primarily monitored during a sunspot minimum in the 1960s. The parabolic antennas are designed to detect radio signals from hydrogen atoms in order to map matter in the Milky Way. The observatory grounds and visitors' centre are open year-round; check signs at the parking area for times. Visitors must walk 400 metres into the site, because car engines interfere with the sensitive instruments in the observatory.

About a kilometre north of the observatory entrance, you'll notice a series of low rock cuts on the east side of the road. Most of the rock is sandy-coloured, but it has distinct blackish veins. The black is essentially coal—the White Lake Basin once had a number of small coal mines in the early 1900s. Unfortunately for the miners, the coal seams were generally small, and the coal contained too much sulphur to command a decent price; the last shipment was made in 1933. But the present attraction of these black veins is the number of fossils they produce. These rocks were laid down as mud and sand along slow-moving rivers or lakeshores

57

in the Eocene Period, when the White Lake area was in the midst of its volcanic activity. The forests at that time were dominated by dawn redwood, a relative of modern sequoias and redwoods that survives in the wild today only in one part of China. Dawn redwoods are deciduous conifers, so the branchlets of needles they shed each fall accumulate on the forest floor and are extremely common in the fossils found in these rock cuts.

The road continues north through ponderosa pine forests and residential acreages, then winds down to meet Highway 97 along a small stream known officially as the Marron River, though it is only a brook flowing in the ditch along the road. *Marron* is a French word meaning "a tame animal that has gone wild"; this river's name refers to the wild horses common in the area. At the highway junction you can turn north to Penticton or south to Okanagan Falls and Oliver. · · · · · · · · · · · · · · · · · · ·

5

BLACK SAGE ROAD AND TUGULNUIT LAKE

35 km, all paved

Black Sage Road is another classic side road of the south Okanagan. It takes you from the north end of Osoyoos Lake along the east side of the valley north past Oliver, rejoining Highway 97 just south of Vaseux Lake.

Start: Junction of Highway 97 and No. 22 Road
between Oliver and Osoyoos.

JUST NORTH OF OSOYOOS LAKE, take No. 22 Road (for some reason known more widely as Road 22 locally) east off Highway 97. The road drops to the floodplain of the Okanagan River, passing through a marshy area marked by growth of cattails and bulrush. In spring this marsh is alive with the braying calls of yellow-headed blackbirds, the raucous quacks of Virginia rails, and the whistled whinnies of soras. Marsh wrens chatter from the bulrushes, their football-shaped nests woven to the stems of the reeds. Like many wrens, male marsh wrens build more than one nest to show off to their female partners. The females choose one and do the interior remodelling themselves, adding soft cattail down to the rough interior before laying their eggs.

Beyond the patches of marsh are moist meadows—hay fields watered by the water table, which is never far below the ground here. In April, long-billed curlews nest on the fields, the birds giving mournful cries to advertise their presence. These large sandpipers become harder to see in May as the grass grows tall; their young grow quickly, and by July both young and old curlews

59

gather in small flocks and leave the valley for coastal wintering grounds in California and Mexico. The taller grass of May attracts bobolinks to the Road 22 meadows, and the black-and-white males are often seen chasing each other and the buff-coloured females over the hay, chattering out the bubbling song that gives them their name. The fields south of the road and immediately east of the highway are being invaded by Russian olives, trees native to southeastern Europe and considered a weed in much of the American West. This is the only spot in Canada where I've noticed them taking over wetland habitat; they grow in more open groves elsewhere in southern British Columbia.

The wet grasslands are filled with unseen meadow mice, and that food supply attracts a steady flow of mouse-hunting birds. A few kestrels—small falcons—are often seen perched on the power lines along the road, intently watching the nearby grass for movement. Red-tailed hawks perch on power poles year-round, joined in winter by rough-legged hawks that have flown south from Arctic nesting grounds. Northern harriers fly back and forth over the meadows on long, narrow wings, listening for mice in the thick growth below; you can easily recognize the harrier by a prominent white patch at the base of its tail. Harriers have a circular ruff of facial feathers, similar to that found in the owl family, which they use to funnel faint sounds into their ears. Barn owls and long-eared owls roost in the dense birch woodlands along the old river channel by day, then replace the harriers on the mouse-hunting night shift. The owls are often joined by coyotes quietly pacing through the grass, their ears cocked, ready to pounce on any squeak.

A small parking lot sits at the south side of the road just before the river bridge. If you have time for a walk, stop here, read the informative kiosk signs, and then stretch your legs along the river

60

dyke. Although most of the land along Road 22 is private, once you've walked a few hundred metres in either direction along the river, you usually have public land beside you.

The road crosses the Okanagan River channel on a narrow bridge; you can usually drive south down the dyke on the east side of the river to Osoyoos Lake, but the other dykes are normally gated and restricted to foot traffic. Okanagan River was channelized in the 1950s to control spring floodwaters; the canal was designed to literally flush the spring runoff through the valley as quickly as possible. Periodic weirs drop the water level in a controlled fashion; these produce extremely dangerous rolling currents, so swimming anywhere near them can be a fatal experience. The old river channel winds back and forth across the valley, its path marked by a thick growth of deciduous trees, mostly water birch mixed with alder. In summer you can see colourful wood ducks and painted turtles in these oxbows. The warm waters are also home to interesting insects; the oxbow on the north side of the road just before the big old barn is one of the few places that the powder-blue western pondhawk has been found in the British Columbia Interior.

The barn and historic ranch houses at the east end of Road 22 are part of the old Haynes Ranch. John Carmichael Haynes was a government agent and later a judge in the early days of Osoyoos; he used his influence to amass about 22,000 acres of ranchland in the area. If you look into the barn from the east side, you might be lucky enough to see a roosting barn owl. These birds have nested in the barn several times since 1990, the first time the species was found breeding in the British Columbia Interior. Barn owls are generally nonmigratory and can't tolerate deep snow, so they are very rare in Canada outside of the southern coast of

61

focus ➤ **Burrowing Owl**

The bird from which Burrowing Owl Estate Winery takes its name is an unusual owl in several ways—it is more diurnal than nocturnal and has long, bare legs and a habit of doing regular knee-bends. But what really sets the burrowing owl apart from its cousins is that it nests and roosts underground, in burrows dug by badgers or other fossorial mammals. Like many other small owls, burrowing owls eat a variety of prey; the local birds generally catch pocket mice in the spring and early summer, then switch to large insects such as beetles and Jerusalem crickets in summer and early autumn. By October the insect numbers dwindle and pocket mice begin to hibernate, so the owls migrate south, probably wintering in California and northern Mexico. They return in late March or early April, and the evening air echoes with the males' *cu-kooo* calls.

Burrowing owls were once fairly common in the Okanagan and south Similkameen valleys, but they declined rapidly in the late 1800s when cattle overgrazed the area, degrading the habitat and likely trampling a lot of the nests in sandy soils. In the 1980s and 1990s, the British Columbia Ministry of Environment attempted to reintroduce these owls to the Okanagan, bringing owl families up from a healthy population in central Washington. Most were released in the grasslands adjacent to Burrowing Owl vineyards. Owl numbers were maintained as long as new recruits were brought in each year, but when imports from south of the border stopped in the early 1990s, the numbers declined quickly. The last burrowing owl was seen here in 1995, three years before the winery produced its first vintage.

British Columbia. If the owls aren't in the barn, you should at least see Say's phoebes flitting around the corrals any time from late February through October. These black-tailed, orange-bellied fly-catchers build nests in the barn's eaves and rafters. Please do not enter the barn—it is dangerously in need of repairs, and I can personally attest to what it feels like to fall through its rotten rafters!

To the east you can see a large, rocky hill called "the Throne." This is part of the Haynes' Lease Ecological Reserve, 101 hectares of land set aside in 1980 to protect some of the desert-like habitats of the south Okanagan. The high cliffs are home to one of the few peregrine falcon pairs that nest in the southern Interior. The reserve extends south from the Throne in a narrow strip to the northern shore of Osoyoos Lake.

Turn north onto Black Sage Road at the T-junction at the end of Road 22. Here you can seen the stark contrast between the lush meadows on the floodplain and the desert grasslands on the sandy benches. The dark, gangly shrubs are antelope brush, and this site marks one of a few remnant patches of this habitat left in the valley. Antelope brush was once widespread from the United States border north to Penticton. Many of the larger shrubs have a warren of small burrows underneath them, the homes of pocket mice. These smaller cousins of kangaroo rats are highly nocturnal, hopping over the sand by night and stuffing seeds into their cheek pouches or pockets. Pocket mice are true hibernators, sleeping away the winter in their underground homes before emerging in mid-March when spring blossoms on the grasslands.

You quickly reach the first large vineyards of Black Sage Road. Burrowing Owl Estate Winery lies across the road from the sandy grasslands of the South Okanagan Wildlife Management Area. Lark sparrows—big, handsome sparrows with striking chestnut faces—sing from the antelope brush, and you can often see an osprey on its nest on a pole towards the river from here.

Through the main vineyard section of Black Sage Road you are naturally surrounded by a vast landscape of grapes. In winter you may sometimes see western bluebirds flashing through the cinnamon-coloured vines, looking for bunches missed during harvest. As the road angles westward onto the sidehill, you'll see that the natural antelope brush vegetation was recently burned—a wildfire swept through here in 2007. Fires are a natural part of these dry grassland and shrub ecosystems, creating a mosaic of different habitat types, some dominated by grasses and others by shrubs. Unfortunately, this system doesn't function properly when habitats are reduced to small patches and separated from similar habitats by large areas of agricultural and suburban landscape. The opportunities for natural reseeding by native plants are greatly reduced if an entire habitat patch burns to the sand. The British Columbia Ministry of Environment set this area aside some years ago to retain a narrow corridor of natural grassland, fully aware that the risk of wildfire might make the task of preservation more difficult.

The road gradually descends to the valley bottom, keeping grasslands and cliffs on the east side and orchards and vineyards on the west. It then turns to climb back onto a flat, sandy bench now planted with vines and corn. This bench is one of many in the valley formed at the end of the Pleistocene Epoch as young meltwater streams brought sand and gravel down from the hills to rest against the glacial ice in the valley bottom. The road descends slightly once again, to meet McKinney Road in a T-junction; turn east for a few metres on McKinney, then resume your northward journey on Boundary Road. This takes you through the suburban outskirts of Oliver, where you'll eventually meet the east side of Tugulnuit

65

{ *Black Sage Road and Tugulnuit Lake* }

Lake. This lake formed when a channel of the Okanagan River was blocked by a large alluvial fan built by Wolfcub Creek flowing in from the east at the end of the last ice age. The river now occupies another channel, west of the lake. Being surrounded by houses, Tugulnuit Lake has almost no natural shoreline, but it can be a good place to look for migrant waterfowl in spring and fall.

The road continues north, past small rural holdings, to meet Highway 97 at the large Jackson-Triggs Winery. Just before the winery on the west side of the road is Inkaneep Provincial Park, a nice spot for a picnic in the shady trees. The park protects a tiny area of native riparian vegetation—birches, cottonwoods, roses, and willows—that harbours a number of endangered species. One of these is the yellow-breasted chat, a relatively large songbird that is bright yellow below and grey above. The chats usually stay well hidden in the cover, but you can easily hear the males on spring mornings (and often all night long) performing their loud, unmusical songs, which consist of loud whistles and rattling trills. The meowing calls coming from the rosebushes belong to the grey catbird, another denizen of these riverside thickets.

From the junction with Highway 97, you can turn left to return to Oliver and Osoyoos or turn right to continue north towards Penticton (section 6). ·

6

NORTH OLIVER TO OKANAGAN FALLS

15 km, all paved

This route goes through one of the most spectacular and naturally diverse landscapes in southern British Columbia.

START: Okanagan River Bridge on Highway 97 about 5 km north of Oliver; drive north on Highway 97.

THIS ROUTE BEGINS at the bridge where Highway 97 crosses the Okanagan River north of Oliver; the junction with Tugulnuit Lake Road is just 100 metres to the east. The view is dominated to the north by the massive face of McIntyre Bluff on the west and another sheer rock face on the east.

The reach of the Okanagan River from here north to McIntyre Bluff is the only Canadian section of the river still in its natural course. This section was not channelized, because it is an important sockeye salmon spawning ground. You can see numbers of these large, scarlet fish in September and October as they jockey for position in the gravelly shallows. They have come all the way from the Pacific Ocean, up the Columbia River, climbing fish ladders over eleven large dams, to spawn at this site as their ancestors have for millennia. This is one of only two large spawning populations of sockeye left in the Columbia system; the other is along the Wenatchee River in Washington. Though no one knows how many salmon spawned here annually before the dams were built, it was probably in the hundreds of thousands. Recent spawning populations have numbered between five and ten thousand, with occasional years of good returns. The latest run (2008) was

67

one of those good years, with more than sixty thousand big, red fish in the river.

There are continuing initiatives to rejuvenate this stock of salmon. One of the most exciting plans is to allow the river to revert back to a more natural channel where possible. This could greatly increase the available spawning area and also encourage the growth of natural riverside vegetation. Not only are these riparian woodlands important for keeping the river water clean and cool, they are one of the most endangered ecosystems in the valley, so any action that would increase their area would be doubly valuable. If you have time, stop and walk or bike down the paved trail along the west side of the river south to Oliver. The wildlife watching along the trail is excellent, even in winter, when you might spot an American dipper bobbing on a midriver rock.

Continuing north, you pass the big rock cliffs on the east side of the road above Gallagher Lake, a small lake obscured behind pines. These cliffs were the first place in Canada where spotted bats were discovered roosting. This bat looks like a tiny flying skunk (though it is big for a local bat), with big white spots on its black fur set off by a pair of huge pink ears. Spotted bats forage over lowland ponderosa pines and cottonwood groves, searching for relatively large flying insects to gobble up. The bats use rather low-pitched sonar clicks to detect these large insects. The sonar clicks of all other Canadian bats are ultrasonic; that is, they are too high-pitched for humans to hear. But spotted bat clicks can be heard quite easily, sounding like high, regularly repeated *chips* above the trees. The discovery of these bats in British Columbia was quite unexpected, but after local naturalists and biologists learned how to identify them by their calls, the known range of the species was soon extended north to Williams Lake.

The enormous face of McIntyre Bluff fills the sky to the west. This cliff and the massive cliffs on the opposite side of the valley are all composed of ancient metamorphic rocks—mostly gneisses. These are among the oldest rocks in British Columbia; their formation is discussed in more detail in "The Building of the Okanagan Valley" in the introduction to this book.

In 1906 McIntyre Bluff had three nesting pairs of peregrine falcons, but by 1922 most of the Okanagan nest sites of this majestic bird were empty and unused. This local population decline was exacerbated by the drastic effects of DDT on the global population of the species in the 1950s and 1960s, and peregrines became extremely rare in the valley in the latter part of the 1900s. With the banning of DDT in the 1970s, hope was raised for the restoration of peregrines around the world. I was therefore surprised and delighted to discover a pair of peregrines nesting on McIntyre Bluff in 2005; if you stop along the highway in midsummer, you might be lucky enough to hear the noisy fledglings soaring with their fast-flying parents.

McIntyre Bluff is the narrowest point in the Okanagan Valley, and here, at the end of the Pleistocene Epoch about 12,000 years ago, a huge ice plug formed. This plug dammed the flow of meltwaters from the north Okanagan, forming Glacial Lake Penticton and forcing the flow north through the Shuswap and Thompson drainages.

69

Just north of McIntyre Bluff is Vaseux Lake (pronounced VASS-oh), the smallest and shallowest lake that the Okanagan River flows through. The word *vaseux* means "muddy" in French; most of the early European place names in the valley came from the French–Canadian voyageurs travelling along the Hudson's Bay Brigade Trail. This lake and its diverse surroundings have been the focus

focus > **Bighorn Sheep**

Vaseux Lake is famous for its herd of bighorn sheep. These spectacular animals are fairly easy to see from fall through spring, when they graze on the grasses above the highway. The older rams have massive curled horns that they display to each other and smash together in dominance contests; the females have shorter, thinner horns. Groups of bighorns formerly crossed the highway here to reach the lakeshore and hay fields at the south end of the lake, but the road mortality was so high that officials erected a high, wire fence to protect the sheep from vehicle collisions. About 450 sheep once roamed on the east side of the Okanagan Valley from Penticton south to Osoyoos, but in the winter of 1999–2000, a bacterial pneumonia epidemic swept through the herd and reduced the population to about 140. The disease was likely passed to the wild sheep by small domestic sheep herds in the area.

Happily, the bighorn population seems to be making a remarkable recovery and now numbers about three hundred. Small herds are often seen from the highway at Vaseux Lake. The females take to the rugged cliffs in May to give birth to their lambs in safety; at the same time, the adult males retreat into the hills to feed on fresh grass as it greens up at higher elevations in the summer. All of the sheep return to the lower grasslands in the fall, and mating takes place in November.

of much of the conservation activity in the south Okanagan for almost a century. In 1923 the lake was designated as a federal bird sanctuary to protect a small wintering flock of trumpeter swans that had been decimated by lead poisoning. The swans, thought at the time to be near extinction, have made a remarkable comeback here and elsewhere (they are much more common as wintering birds on the British Columbia coast). You can expect to see flocks of swans—both trumpeter and the slightly smaller tundra species—at the north end of the lake every winter, as long as the lake isn't totally frozen.

Large numbers of ducks and geese use the lake as a migratory stopover and wintering site. At one time, the Canada goose population on this lake was a noted local asset, before the species became largely nonmigratory and learned to feed at city parks, golf courses, and school grounds. Birders come to Vaseux Lake from all over the continent because of the amazing habitat diversity—lake, river, marsh, grassland, cliffs, and forest. The cliffs along the lake are home to several interesting birds. Canyon wrens sing their extraordinary cascading song from huge boulders, chukar partridge cackle from the clifftops, and golden eagles soar on updrafts overhead. The rocks are also a favourite spot for reptiles such as western rattlesnakes, gopher snakes, rubber boas, and western skinks.

A large area on the hillsides east of Vaseux Lake burned in the summer of 2003. At that time, a huge fire was burning just south of Kelowna, and some of the major power lines to the city had been cut. The small power line running along the highway at Vaseux Lake became overloaded, and on a hot, windy August day, the line drooped and shorted out to a tree beside the road. The ensuing fire raced north and east, consuming most of the pine forests and

71

grasslands in its path. The grey skeletons of burned antelope brush are conspicuous above the highway.

Recent conservation efforts have made the Vaseux Lake area the most protected area in the bottom of the Okanagan Valley. The west side of the lake, as well as large parcels of land on the east side, are now part of the Vaseux–Bighorn National Wildlife Area, and the Nature Trust of British Columbia also has numerous holdings here. There is a small provincial campground near the north end of the lake, and just beyond is a parking area marked "Vaseux Lake Wildlife Centre." A kiosk provides information on local natural history and conservation, and a boardwalk leads from the parking lot to a bird blind overlooking the marsh. This is a good spot to watch swans and geese in fall, winter, and spring.

From the north end of the lake, you can continue along Highway 97 to Okanagan Falls, or, for a more back-road route, turn northeast at Oliver Ranch Road, which passes numerous wineries and also brings you to the outskirts of Okanagan Falls. If you continue along the highway, you'll pass the Vaseux Lake Bird Observatory about a kilometre north of the lake on the west side of the highway. Watch for parked cars and an inconspicuous gate—the observatory is down a short hill and is really no more than a trailer, a covered table, and a group of dedicated volunteers who monitor the fall bird migration through the area. It operates every morning in August and September and is well worth a stop. A series of mist nets allows a trained biologist to examine the birds for their age, sex, and condition before he or she bands and releases them.

From Okanagan Falls you can continue north to Penticton along Highway 97, return to Oliver via Green Lake Road (section 7), or go north to Penticton along Eastside Road (section 9). · ·

72

7

GREEN LAKE ROAD

13 km, all paved

This route takes you from Okanagan Falls south along the Okanagan River, then into the hills and past a series of small lakes to meet Fairview–White Lake Road (section 4) at Willowbrook.

START: Junction of Green Lake Road and Highway 97, just west of the bridge over the Okanagan River in Okanagan Falls; turn south onto Green Lake Road.

———

THERE NEVER WAS much of a waterfall at Okanagan Falls, just a rocky gap where Skaha Lake emptied into the Okanagan River. The Syilx name for this site was Kwak-ne-ta, or "little falls." A small dam, built on the site of the falls in the 1950s, regulates the depth of Skaha Lake. The rocks here are volcanic, created as the Okanagan Valley cracked open about 55 million years ago. The falls acted as a barrier that slowed the sockeye salmon migrating north into Skaha Lake and were an important gathering place for Native peoples in the autumn as they harvested the bright red fish. According to local elders, the Native villages between Okanagan Falls and Vaseux Lake were once the largest in the south Okanagan.

The dam now completely blocks the movement of salmon into Skaha Lake. A ten-year study assessing the impact on the local kokanee population of reintroducing sockeye is nearly complete. The kokanee are a landlocked form of sockeye that live in the lake throughout their lives instead of migrating to the ocean. If the impacts are judged to be minimal, fisheries biologists will create

73

a working fish ladder to allow the oceangoing sockeye to enter Skaha Lake and spawn in the creeks and river at Penticton.

Another attraction at the falls are the dippers. These small songbirds look like grey tennis balls as they bob up and down on the rocks in the river. They "dip" by diving into the strong current, foraging for insect larvae on the river bottom. Dippers traditionally nest on cliffs next to waterfalls; here they use the dam sluice gates to support their mossy nests. More arrive on the scene in winter, and you can sometimes see five or ten in the first few hundred metres of the river. A flock of goldeneyes joins the dippers from October through April, diving for aquatic invertebrates in the fast water. Both Barrow's and common goldeneyes are in this flock; the black-and-white drakes are easily identified by their facial spots—a round spot on the common, a crescent on the Barrow's.

Okanagan Falls Provincial Park, a small campsite just around the corner, is a nice spot to stop for a few minutes or a few days. One of the most impressive wildlife spectacles here happens at night. In summer the river below the outlet dam comes alive with flying insects—mayflies, stoneflies, and caddisflies emerging from their pupae, then dancing above the water to begin the mating cycle again. This cloud of insects attracts a cloud of insect-eating birds and bats as darkness falls. Hundreds of common nighthawks crisscross over the water, and dozens of tiny bats of several species flutter around.

The road winds south along the base of the steep mountainside, staying close to the river for the first 3 or 4 kilometres. The river was channelized in the 1950s to control water flow out of the valley; you can see a number of weirs across the river that drop the water level in a regular fashion. Large Douglas-firs grow out of rocky talus slopes; they survive by tapping into ground water

74

focus ❭ **Bluebirds**

The Okanagan is home to two species of bluebird: the western bluebird and the mountain bluebird. Western bluebirds are common in the open pine forests along Green Mountain Road; if you'd like to see mountain bluebirds, turn north at the end of the road and drive to the open grasslands of White Lake (section 4). The male western is a deep purplish-blue with a rusty breast; the male mountain is solid sky-blue. The greyer females are harder to tell apart, but the female western always has a trace of rust on the breast.

Both species declined in the mid-1900s as European starlings expanded across North America. These aggressive newcomers took over the old woodpecker holes and other tree cavities used by the nesting bluebirds. Bird lovers responded by erecting nest boxes for the bluebirds, with openings too small for the starlings. There are now thousands of boxes on fence posts and trees throughout the grasslands and open woodlands of North America; these "bluebird trails" are monitored and maintained by an army of enthusiastic volunteers. Both species of bluebirds may well be commoner now than ever, since significant habitat losses have been countered by the increase in nest sites.

that flows downhill over the bedrock. About 3 kilometres from the highway, the river channel bends away from the road. The large, wet meadow and marsh on the west side of the river is part of the Vaseux–Bighorn National Wildlife Area. Channels and ponds have been recently dug into the meadow to create moist woodland habitat for various endangered species, including the yellow-breasted chat. Over the next few decades, these areas will mature into a mosaic of rose thickets and birch woodlands similar to the small patches seen on the east side of the floodplain.

The road climbs very steeply around a couple of switchback corners to the vineyards of See Ya Later Ranch. This ranch was the site of some of the earliest commercial grape plantings in the Okanagan. Watch for western bluebirds around the vineyard, particularly in winter, when the indigo-coloured birds rely on the sweet leftover grapes for survival.

Around the next corner is Green Lake, which likely gets its colour from white calcium carbonate crystals suspended in its waters and collected on its bottom. This produces a colour similar to those seen in glacial lakes filled with fine glacial silt. Green Lake has no fish, but it attracts a variety of diving ducks in fall and spring migration that feed on a good supply of aquatic invertebrates.

Just past Green Lake the road swings westward, and you can see Sleeping Waters Lake in the woods to the south. This private lake has a population of tiger salamanders that are paedomorphic—they remain in their gilled, larval-like form while growing and becoming sexually mature. These totally aquatic amphibians can become quite large and are the naturally dominant predator in many of the small lakes in the south Okanagan that lack water outlets and, therefore, have no fish. Unfortunately, trout have

76

been introduced to many of these lakes for sportfishing, often after government biologists poisoned the lakes to remove both salamanders and the introduced nongame fish that would compete with the trout. These populations of tiger salamanders are therefore now very rare, and the species is listed as endangered in British Columbia.

The next lake in the neighbourhood is Mahoney Lake, a horseshoe-shaped body of water that, like many small lakes in this area, has no outlet. Although it is fed only by spring runoff from the surrounding hills and occasional summer rains, Mahoney Lake is deep—about 18 metres deep—and never dries up like White Lake (section 4). It lies over alkaline lava, and its waters, particularly those near the bottom, are very salty. The upper parts of its water column are clear and full of life—plankton thrive, and ducks flock to the lake to feed on the plankton. All of this seems typical of many lakes, but Mahoney is strikingly different from most of those small lakes and, indeed, most lakes in the world.

Mahoney Lake is strongly meromictic, meaning its waters don't mix seasonally like those of most other lakes. This lack of mixing is likely caused by the high bluffs that protect the lake from prevailing winds from the north and, to a lesser extent, from the south. The water near the surface receives oxygen from the atmosphere, but almost none reaches the deeper waters, since the upper layers never mix with the lower ones. Between these two water layers—at a depth of about 6 metres—is a remarkable plate of sulphur bacteria that extends across the lake—a bright pink, porridge-like blanket that divides the sunlit, oxygenated waters above from the black, anaerobic world below. These bacteria use sulphur instead of oxygen to fuel their cellular energy circuits. Mahoney Lake is world famous among aquatic scientists because of this feature.

From Mahoney Lake, the road drops slightly into the Kearns Creek valley. Kearns Creek is fed by many springs, so parts of it have open water year-round. Marsh-loving birds such as Wilson's snipe and Virginia rail can therefore be found here in winter, although they are absent from some of the larger marshes in the valley at that time. After travelling through the northern edge of the rural community of Willowbrook, Green Lake Road meets Fairview–White Lake Road (section 4). You can turn right here (north) to go to White Lake and on to Penticton or Keremeos, or turn south to Oliver. · · · · · · · · · · · · · · · · · ·

{ 8 }

PENTICTON TO KEREMEOS

41 km, all paved highway

*This route takes you from Penticton south to Kaleden on
Highway 97, then through the Yellow Lake pass to Keremeos
in the Similkameen Valley on Highway 3A.*

START: Highway 97 at Skaha Lake, south Penticton;
drive west and south on Highway 97.

YOU LEAVE PENTICTON along the natural sand beaches of Skaha
Lake. The city of Penticton is built on the deltas of three creeks:
Shingle Creek coming from the west, Ellis Creek from the east,
and Penticton Creek from the northeast. The first two of these
creeks enter the Okanagan River channel from opposite sides halfway between Okanagan and Skaha Lakes, and for millennia their
sand has been deposited where the river empties into Skaha Lake.
Penticton Creek empties into Okanagan Lake, so its sands contrib-
ute to the beaches on the north side of Penticton. Without these
deltaic deposits, Skaha Lake would simply be the south end of
Okanagan Lake, and Penticton would be deep underwater.

The highway turns south and climbs gently to start a long
traverse of the steep hillsides west of Skaha Lake. It first travels
through silts deposited by Glacial Lake Penticton at the end of
the Pleistocene Epoch about 12,000 years ago. If you look care-
fully at some of these silt bluffs, you can see that they are made
up of a series of horizontal layers, called varves. Each of these layers was laid down in a single year; they grew fastest in summer,
when meltwaters carried silt into the lake. Some of the bluffs have

79

{ Penticton to Keremeos }

focus ➤ **Barrow's Goldeneye**

You can almost always see a few ducks on Yellow Lake; the commonest species is the Barrow's goldeneye. These ducks winter on the Pacific coast, where they feed largely on mussels. In April they fly inland to nest on lakes scattered throughout the mountains and plateaus of British Columbia—the province hosts more than half the world's population. The handsome males are boldly patterned in black and white and marked with a distinctive white crescent on the face. The females have grey bodies and brown heads but sport a bright yellow-orange bill in breeding season.

Goldeneyes are diving ducks, and in summer they feed on aquatic insects, shrimp, and other invertebrates. Like all varieties of duck, the goldeneye male leaves all nesting and brood-rearing tasks to the female. She chooses a large cavity in a tree for her nest, usually one excavated by a pileated woodpecker. If she can't find a tree nest, she may opt for a hole in a cliff; one local goldeneye even nested in an unused marmot burrow. The black-and-white fluffball young jump out of the cavity within a day of hatching, sometimes falling as far as 20 metres to the ground, where they bounce and quickly run to the water with their mother. Like most ducks, goldeneye pairs were once thought to be faithful for only a single season, since the males leave the females as soon as they have finished laying the full clutch of eggs. But a detailed study in British Columbia using marked birds showed that many couples found each other again on the wintering grounds and nested together the following spring.

clusters of small holes bored into them; these are the nest burrows of bank swallows. These small, brown swallows—with their distinctive brown breastbands—return each year from their wintering grounds in South America to feed on the abundant insect life over the lake and river.

If you pull into the viewpoint on the east side of the highway near the top of the hill, you might see a second species of swallow—the violet-green. These birds nest in rock crevices in the bluffs across the road; they are one of the earliest migrants to return in spring, probably because they travel only as far as California and Mexico for the winter.

The rocks here are largely volcanic, formed during the birth of the Okanagan Valley about 55 million years ago. On the other side of Skaha Lake, you can see the pale cliffs known widely among the climbing fraternity as the Skaha Bluffs. Those rocks are much older than the ones you are driving by on the west side. The Skaha Bluffs are metamorphic rock, gneiss, initially laid down as sedimentary rock on the continental shelf of North America, perhaps as long as 2 billion years ago. Then about 180 million years ago, an arc of large islands collided with the Pacific coast of North America, burying the shelf sediments under kilometres of rock. Under this tremendous pressure and heat, the shelf rocks melted and recrystallized as gneiss. They reappeared when the valley opened up many millennia later.

As the highway levels off, it begins to pass the orchards and fruit stands of Kaleden on the east side of the road and rangeland on the west side. This rangeland is severely overgrazed by wild horses—the contrast between the ungrazed grass on the highway side of the fence and the stubble on the west side is quite striking. In spring, bright yellow balsamroot flowers beam from the less-grazed areas. As you approach the junction with Highway 3A, the habitat changes to an open ponderosa pine forest with antelope brush growing beneath. These shrubs, members of the rose family, are covered with pale yellow blossoms in late April and early May.

Turn west at the junction to follow Highway 3A. The road curves through the birch-and-alder-filled gully of the Marron River (rather ostentatiously named, as it is less than a metre wide), then winds up a steep hill known locally as Roadhouse Hill. The hill is not named after a historical roadhouse on an old stagecoach route but after the Roadhouse family, who once lived in a house at the bottom of the hill. From the top of the hill you can look north to broad slopes covered with sagebrush grasslands; this is the northernmost extensive area of sagebrush in the Okanagan Valley, and similarly the northern limit to sagebrush-dependent species such as the Brewer's sparrow. The hillside on the south side of the highway is Mount Parker; it was formerly cloaked in a dense Douglas-fir forest, but most of this burned in a large forest fire in 1984. The layered cliffs of Mount Parker, easily visible a few kilometres farther on, are more of the volcanic formations mentioned earlier, lava flows that filled the basin several thousand metres deep.

At the top of Roadhouse Hill, you enter the broader section of the Marron Valley, once part of the important Hudson's Bay Brigade Trail route. Fur traders travelled north from Osoyoos to Oliver, then through the White Lake Basin to Twin Lakes and the Marron Valley, continuing north via Shingle Creek to Summerland. The road climbs another slope, skirting the south shore of Trout Lake, then passing the junction with the Twin Lakes Road. The golf course here is probably the only one in existence that takes the yellow-bellied marmot as its mascot. These large "groundhogs" are very common in the rocky grasslands, and the golfers undertook an unsuccessful battle against them when the course was first set up. The victorious marmots now symbolize the course and even appear on the clubhouse menu as the "famous Marmot Burger" (presumably not marmot in origin). Marmots are large members of the squirrel family and are true hibernators, sleeping in their underground burrows from late summer through the winter and emerging with the first shoots of green grass in the spring.

If you turn south at the Twin Lakes junction, you will end up at White Lake (section 4), but we will continue on the highway, which enters a narrow, rocky valley before reaching Yellow Lake. This lake has no natural fish population, since its waters normally contain insufficient oxygen for fish to survive the winter, when a thick layer of ice covers the lake's surface. An aerator was installed in 1977 to alleviate the problem, and after a few initial adjustments, the introduction of rainbow and brook trout has been successful, at least from a sportfishing perspective. At first the aerator was set too deep in the water, and it brought anoxic water and poisonous hydrogen sulphide to the surface, killing the introduced fish. It was also initially operated in the winter, in order to provide oxygen below the ice. However, the biologists found that aeration in the fall and early winter was sufficient, since it served to turn the upper water layers over, bringing surface oxygen to the deeper waters. The lake is now one of the most popular fishing lakes in the province, particularly in winter, when its surface is dotted with keen ice fishers. But ecosystem changes like this always also create losers; the introduction of fish eliminated a large population of tiger salamanders—now an endangered species—from the lake.

Yellow Lake is at 760 metres elevation, and its narrow valley provides a good example of the effect of aspect on vegetation. The hillsides south of the lake, shaded for much of the day, are cloaked

83

in a cool Douglas-fir forest, while the sunny slopes to the north are open grasslands dotted with sagebrush. At Yellow Lake you leave the Okanagan Valley as the road drops steeply into the Keremeos Creek drainage, part of the Similkameen system. Keremeos Creek comes out of a very narrow valley on the northwest side of the highway, marked by a line of large, veteran cottonwood trees, then winds across hay fields to the east.

Just north of the hamlet of Olalla (named after the Chinook jargon word for "berry"—*olallie*—because of the prevalence of saskatoon berries in this area), watch for mountain goats on the rocky cliffs west of the highway. Their white fur stands out (in summer, at least) against the rocks. Also watch the gravel road cuts on the west side of the road for a distinct layer of white soil. This is ash from the eruption of Mount Mazama in Oregon. This huge volcano blew up about 7,000 years ago, creating what is now known as Crater Lake. The ash spread over much of western North America, and geologists and archaeologists everywhere use it to date rocks or artifacts found just above or below it.

You leave Olalla almost as quickly as you enter it and are now on the northern outskirts of Keremeos. In the southern distance, you can see the talus slopes forming a huge letter "K," the symbol of the town. From Keremeos you can turn west to follow Highway 3 to Vancouver, or turn east and south to follow the same highway to Osoyoos. · · · · · · · · · · · · · · · · · ·

focus ⟩ **Western Screech-Owl**

The western screech-owl is one of many species in the Okanagan Valley that are restricted to riparian ecosystems and have declined significantly because of the loss of that habitat. This small owl, about 20 centimetres long and weighing about 200 grams, is considered endangered in the British Columbia Interior and is declining rapidly on the southern coast of the province as well. Recent surveys suggest that between one and two hundred pairs live in the Interior, resident along well-treed stretches of rivers and creeks in the Okanagan and Kootenay valleys.

Screech-owls are generalist predators, eating everything from mice and small birds to beetles, slugs, worms, frogs, and fish. One of the reasons they like mature riparian woodlands is the abundance of cavities in cottonwoods, birches, and aspen, trees favoured by woodpeckers because they quickly form soft, somewhat rotten cores. The owls nest and roost in these cavities, although they also roost in thickly leaved trees such as western redcedar. Western screech-owls are highly nocturnal and are usually detected only by their distinctive calls. One of these calls is a descending series of hollow whistles that speeds up towards the end, patterned like the taps of a bouncing ball. Another common call is a two-parted trill that a pair uses to keep in touch with each other. Like most owls, the female has a higher-pitched voice than the male, even though her body is significantly larger than his.

9

MCLEAN CREEK AND EASTSIDE ROAD

17 km, all paved

This route provides a nice alternative to Highway 97 if
you are travelling between Okanagan Falls and Penticton.
The McLean Creek valley is an area of small farms and ranches
tucked out of sight behind a low range of hills; the north part
of the route travels along the eastern shore of Skaha Lake.

START: Intersection of 10th Avenue and Highway 97 (Main Street) in downtown Okanagan Falls; turn east at 10th Avenue.

AS YOU LEAVE town on 10th Avenue and the road turns into McLean Creek Road, apple and pear orchards quickly appear on the north side of the road, which climbs onto the rolling bench below the towering orange cliffs of Peach Bluff. This rock wall is home to a small number of bighorn sheep and a few species of birds restricted to rugged terrain. Canyon wrens sing their cascading, whistled songs from the cliffs, and chukars cackle from the talus slopes along the bottom of the hill. Occasionally peregrine falcons nest on the bluff ledges. The talus slopes are dotted with saskatoon bushes, and thick clusters of Oregon grape grow at their bases.

86

To the south you can see the industrial sprawl of the large Weyerhaeuser sawmill; this operation closed in late 2007 when lumber prices tumbled in North America. The road turns sharply north as it reaches the flat bench formed by gravel deposits from McLean and Shuttleworth creeks. The more adventurous can turn eastward at Allendale Lake Road, which joins our route just

Hot sun and warm water draw swimmers to Okanagan
beaches such as this one in Penticton, at Skaha Lake.

Brittle prickly pear cacti bloom in June,
each waxy yellow flower lasting for only a single day.

American coots form large flocks on Okanagan Lake in winter.

The yellow-headed blackbird is a striking
resident of rich marshes in the Okanagan Valley.

Bluebunch wheatgrass is the archetypal bunchgrass of the West.

These rock bluffs at White Lake were created
during intense volcanic activity about 50 million years ago.

Native people drew these pictographs at Vaseux Lake with red ochre,
likely brought in from the Princeton area, 100 kilometres to the west.

This view of Osoyoos Lake from the east shows the clear difference between the irrigated farmlands and dry, native grasslands.

Badgers were once common predators throughout the grasslands but are now listed as endangered in British Columbia.

The remarkable circles in Spotted Lake are formed from
epsom salts—mostly magnesium and sodium sulphates.

A chukar, a partridge native to the dry mountains of Eurasia, runs across the road to find cover on a rocky hillside.

This large boulder just north of the Chopaka–Nighthawk border crossing is an erratic, dropped by a receding glacier thousands of years ago

Snowshoe hares are residents of the coniferous forests at high elevations in the Okanagan.

A Great Basin spadefoot retreats into loose soil,
where it can hide from predators and the hot summer sun.

Like other alkaline ponds, White Lake has no
outlet—its waters simply evaporate away.

Faced with an intruder, a young long-eared owl
tries to look as big and menacing as possible.

A western pondhawk suns on a leaf; in the British
Columbia Interior this dragonfly is known only from the river
oxbows at the north end of Osoyoos Lake.

The massive rocks of McIntyre Bluff are made of gneiss,
metamorphic rock that recrystallized deep underground.

American dippers are common along Okanagan streams,
especially those in which kokanee salmon spawn.

Peregrine falcons were essentially absent from the Okanagan
for several decades, but now fly again over the valley.

This common yellowthroat was banded
at the Vaseux Lake Bird Observatory.

north of this sharp turn; this road bounces into the high country above Okanagan Falls to a small lake in subalpine forests at about 1,550 metres elevation.

Continue north on McLean Creek Road as it hugs the western edge of the bench. The hills are clad in young ponderosa pines with an understory of antelope brush, and a line of big old cottonwoods marks the path of McLean Creek, winding its way across the hay fields east of the road. As the road rounds the east side of the hill, the pines give way to Douglas-firs growing on the shadier north side, many of them bearing large "witches' brooms" of dense twigs, the sign of dwarf mistletoe attack.

The road eventually makes a sharp S-bend across the narrowing valley, crossing McLean Creek and continuing northwest along the other side. The valley narrows still more as the road begins to descend; the creek is lined with water birch and old cottonwoods, a rare patch of mature riparian woodland. Riparian (from the Latin *ripa*, meaning riverbank) habitat is one of the most endangered in the valley, since housing developments and agricultural operations almost always occur first alongside creeks, rivers, and lakeshores.

The road levels out as McLean Creek nears Skaha Lake, and you soon reach the junction with Eastside Road. Turn right (north) towards Penticton; a left turn will take you back to Okanagan Falls. Within a few hundred metres, the road drops to lake level. You will start to see silt bluffs on the east side of the road. The whitish silt was deposited in the bottom of Glacial Lake Penticton when it was dammed by an ice plug south of Vaseux Lake at the end of the Pleistocene Epoch about 12,000 years ago. Watch for clusters of small holes burrowed into the silt; these are bank swallow nest holes.

About 3 kilometres north of the McLean Creek junction, you will begin to see exposures of rock marked with dark and light bands. This is gneiss, a metamorphic rock formed during the deep burial of continental shelf sediments almost 200 million years ago. The rock reemerged when the Okanagan Valley cracked open about 55 million years ago, and the fractured landscape on the northeast side of Skaha Lake is now one of the most popular rock-climbing sites in North America. It is also favoured by big-horn sheep, which use the rocks as escape terrain and graze on the native grasslands on the lower hills. Much of the hills above you have been set aside by the provincial government and various con-servation agencies to protect the sheep and other species restricted to these dry, rocky habitats.

Look closely at the silty hillsides you pass on your way north. You should see white deposits of salt that have leached out of the soil by water flowing through the silt from above. The large clumps of coarse grass growing here are wild rye, a species that prefers these alkaline soils. The water flowing through the silt ren-ders them somewhat unstable, and some houses along this road have had to be abandoned because of slumping slopes above.

As you enter the city of Penticton and begin to drive through housing developments, you'll see rocky outcrops along the east side of the road. Watch these closely for spectacular clumps of brit-tle prickly pear cactus. These low mats produce big, yellow flower clusters in June. Each flower lasts for only a day. · · · · · · ·

88

10

APEX MOUNTAIN AND GREEN MOUNTAIN ROAD

33 km, all paved secondary road

*This is the road to the main ski area in the south Okanagan;
it begins in a shady creek valley, then snakes up through a variety
of forest types to the subalpine. An optional route continues on to
Highway 3 at Hedley, or you can retrace your steps to Penticton.*

START: Intersection of Fairview Road and
Channel Parkway (Highway 97) in Penticton; travel west
over the bridge and on to Green Mountain Road.

YOU CAN SEE SHINGLE CREEK entering the Okanagan River just
north of the bridge; Ellis Creek enters the river behind you on
the east side. The deltas of these two creeks provide much of the
land that Penticton is built on. The road winds through the main
village of the Penticton Indian Reserve for the first 2 kilometres.
According to local elders, the main Native village in this part of
the valley used to be located at Vaseux Lake, but after the population was devastated by disease with the arrival of Europeans, the
remaining families joined people already living at Penticton.

To the north you can see a good stand of old cottonwoods;
these trees are one of the last remnants of a major wetland that
covered the northwest corner of Penticton before the Okanagan
River was channelized in the 1950s. The river used to meander
through the western part of Penticton, first through a large marsh
at the north end, then through rich riparian woodlands of cottonwood and water birch. After the river was confined to the channel
dykes, most of the wetland was filled for housing developments,

89

> *black swift*

focus › **Swifts**

Vaux's swifts nest and roost in hollow trees, and cottonwoods are their favourites. Their eastern cousins, chimney swifts, nest in large chimneys, a habit they picked up quickly after the old-growth forests of eastern North America were liquidated during European settlement. Chimney swift populations have declined drastically in the last few decades as usable chimneys disappear from the landscape. Fears of a similar fate have been expressed about Vaux's swifts, since the big, hollow trees they need are becoming rarer each year.

Swifts are small, cigar-shaped birds with swept-back wings. They twinkle through the air while their open mouths scoop up small insects. Their closest relatives are the hummingbirds; both groups have legs that are too small for walking or hopping. The other characteristic that ties them together is wing structure. In most birds the main flight feathers are attached to the ulna, or forearm; the feathers attached to the hand of the wing are used for propulsion. In hummingbirds and swifts, the ulna is so short that the feathers attached to it play little role in flight, but the feathers attached to the hand of the wing are used for both propulsion and lift. This structure allows hummingbirds to hover and gives swifts their distinctive twinkling flight pattern.

There are two other species of swifts in the Okanagan Valley. The all-dark black swift is the largest; it nests on rocky ledges beside mountain waterfalls and forages for flying ants over mountain peaks. The white-throated swift nests in deep crevices on the dry, rocky cliffs throughout the valley.

and the cut-off river bends, or oxbows, lost much of their adjacent woodlands. The cottonwoods have been home to a colony of great blue herons since 2008, but the large, stick nests are difficult to see from the road.

To the south you can see a long, grassy ridge with a lot of small pine trees on its northern flanks. This ridge, and much of the mountain to the south, was burned in a fire in the early 1980s, and reseeding by ponderosa pine is very slow in this hot, dry environment. As you leave the village, the Shingle Creek valley begins to narrow, and you can see white silt hoodoos eroded out of the bench to the south and similar bluffs on the north side. These are composed of glaciolacustrine silts, a term used for the fine glacial flour deposited into lake bottoms. They formed at the end of the Pleistocene Epoch about 12,000 years ago, when ice sheets on the plateau were melting, sending silt, sand, and gravel into the large glacial lake at Penticton.

The valley narrows even further, the creek hemmed in by rock walls at several places. At one point there is a pink-orange cliff on the south side of the road, with obvious, large crystals embedded in it. These crystals are feldspar and quartz in volcanic and igneous rocks formed about 52 million years ago, when the valley was splitting open and molten rocks flowed to the surface.

The creek flows swiftly past these cliffs, and with some luck you might spot an American dipper bobbing on the rocks. These song birds look like grey tennis balls doing knee-bends as they match the water flow with their jerky movements. Dippers forage underwater for insect larvae, swimming against the current with their stubby wings. With even more luck, you might see harlequin ducks here in the spring. These ducks spend most of the year in the Pacific surf along the British Columbia coast but fly to creeks and rivers

in the Interior in April and May to nest. The males are spectacular in slate-blue plumage marked with bright white and chestnut
stripes; the females are a dark brown, with two white smudges on
their cheeks that only make them more difficult to see as they swim
along the dark shores of the creek. British Columbia is home to a
good percentage of the world's harlequin duck population, but few
nests have been found here. The females tuck themselves away in
root tangles along the streambank, and only the luckiest naturalists
have discovered the down-covered eggs. Interestingly, two of the
earliest harlequin duck nests discovered in western North America
were found by anglers fishing along Shingle Creek.

The Shingle Creek valley is an oasis of moist, cool forests in
a hot region. As you cross the first bridge over the creek, you'll
see the red stems of red-osier dogwood shrubs under the trees, a
species typical of creeksides and other wet areas. Unlike other dog-
woods, it doesn't have showy flower clusters framed in large white
bracts but instead has sprays of small white flowers that produce
cream-coloured berries much favoured by birds.

Another plant that requires a high water table is the western
redcedar; you can see a few of these elegant trees scattered along
the creek. There used to be many more large redcedars here;
indeed, the creek gets its name from the shingles cut from the big
trees felled in the early 1900s.

The shady south side of the valley is cloaked in Douglas-fir,
many of the trees bearing large masses of twiggy witches' brooms.
These growths are caused by the attack of dwarf mistletoe, a tiny
parasite that attaches itself to the branches and, in doing so, stim-
ulates the rapid growth of small branches. The energy the tree
puts into the witches' brooms does slow its growth, but the clumps

provide ideal cover for roosting birds, and owls and hawks will even nest on large, thick clumps.

The deciduous woodlands along the creek attract a tremendous diversity of plants and animals, all drawn by the promise of water, cool shade, and abundant food. Summer mornings ring with the exquisite song of the veery; the spiralling cascade of notes perfectly fits the streamside location. The veery is one of three species of drab little thrushes in this region whose voice easily trumps its looks. You might hear the other two—Swainson's and hermit thrushes—higher up on this road. Many large cottonwoods still grow along Shingle Creek, and some of them show the hollow, rotten cores so valued by mammals and birds for home sites. One of the species restricted to this habitat in the British Columbia Interior is the Vaux's swift, the western equivalent of the chimney swift.

Just past the second bridge crossing the creek, the valley opens to a broad, wet meadow. The creek can meander more across the flats, and beavers often choose this spot to dam the stream to deepen the water for their winter navigation needs. Cattails form a lush marsh along one of the old streambeds, and sandbar willows create a thicket nearby. The meadow is used for wintering cattle, and bald eagles gather here in February, during calving season, to feed on the afterbirths. These fields also attract coyotes, which lope through the grass listening for mice. Across the field you can see a big bank swallow colony—a cluster of holes dug into a silt bank.

The Shingle Creek valley swings north at this point, and the road leaves it, turning south up the Shatford Creek valley. After winding past some hay fields, the road crosses the creek and angles westward again to follow the valley. A large volcanic bluff, called Hedges Butte, is prominent to the south. This valley was the old

93

stagecoach route out of Penticton in the late 1800s and early 1900s. Passengers bound for Keremeos and the Hedley gold mines would rest near here at Allen Grove, the first stop on the trip out of Penticton. The hills to the south are heavily cloaked in Douglas-fir, and if you stop here on a summer morning, you might hear the songs of Swainson's thrushes coming from the cool forests, spiralling upwards instead of down like that of the veery.

You soon reach the junction of Green Mountain Road and Apex Mountain Road. You can follow the former to the left, which will take you out to Highway 3A just north of Keremeos, but we will turn right on to Apex Road, following the route of Shatford Creek as it tumbles off the mountain. The road climbs steeply along the north side of the creek through open Douglas-fir forests. Across the creek, the shady north-facing slopes take on a more subalpine character, with Engelmann spruce becoming common, and eventually you are surrounded by this cool, fragrant forest. Spire-like subalpine firs mix with the straight, thin trunks of lodgepole pine, and if you stop to listen, you might hear the high, buzzy songs of Townsend's warblers coming from the treetops in summer. This is also the domain of the hermit thrush, the third member of the trio of masterful singing thrushes. The song of the hermit thrush is the most ethereal of the three, always beginning with a high, pure note, then slipping up or down the scale.

Just before you reach the ski village, you drive through Rock Oven Pass at about 1,760 metres elevation. If you stop and listen here, you might hear the nasal *enk!* of a pika calling from the talus slopes below the road. Pikas are common denizens of the rocky talus slopes at Rock Oven Pass. They are relatives of rabbits and hares but lack the long ears and big hind feet. They spend their summers gathering grass and flowers, curing their harvest in hay piles on sunny rocks, then storing it underground for winter consumption. The jumbled rocks provide easy cover from predators such as hawks and an ample choice of underground accommodation for a cozy winter nest.

The closest relatives of these small "rock rabbits" at this elevation are snowshoe hares, which are, in many ways, the keystone species in this ecosystem. The hares go through ten-year population cycles; at the peak of each cycle, you can see them constantly as you drive along, bounding across the road into the forest. But their predators—great horned owls, northern goshawks, and lynx are the most important—soon catch up with them. The predators raise so many healthy young while the hares are abundant that within two years the hunters literally eat all the hares they can find, and the population declines to the point where it's hard to find a hare anywhere. The predators then turn their attentions to grouse, squirrels, and other prey, allowing the hares to slowly recover in numbers.

When you reach the ski village, you can see the high subalpine ridge of Beaconsfield Mountain to the south and west. This is the hill with the ski runs; the true alpine tundra of Apex Mountain is just out of sight to the south. Any time of year, the most conspicuous birds around the village are members of the crow and jay family. Grey jays, also known as Canada jays or whisky jacks, float among the trees, looking for a well-stocked bird feeder or a skier having lunch. They are often joined by bright blue Steller's jays. Jays have a high degree of intelligence, an important characteristic for year-round survival at this elevation. They spend the summer and fall storing food for winter use, which explains how they ate your lunch so quickly—it's all been tucked away in a tree somewhere. Another common member of this family is the

95

Clark's nutcracker, which looks superficially like a grey jay but has black-and-white wings and a long, woodpecker-like beak. Nut-crackers specialize in storing pine seeds for winter and spring consumption, but they won't turn their noses up at peanuts, either. The largest member of the crow family in the mountains is the common raven. These big birds look for larger scraps—the carrion left by lynx and cougar usually gets them through the winter—but these days they forage a lot in garbage dumps.

The ski village marks the end of the paved road, but you can continue on the Nickel Plate Road if you wish. This gravel road crosses the plateau to the Mascot Mine, then drops in spectacu-lar fashion into the Similkameen Valley, reaching Highway 3 just south of Hedley. Take this road as well if you'd like to hike up Apex Mountain itself; the four-wheel-drive trail starts at the sharp bend just east of the Nickel Plate Cross-Country Ski Area. It is about an 8-kilometre walk to the top of the mountain, a great destination on a hot summer day. · · · · · · · · · · · · · · · · ·

11

NARAMATA ROAD

23 km, all paved

*Naramata Road winds north on orchard-
and vineyard-covered benches from Penticton
to the village of Naramata.*

START: Intersection of Main Street
and Front Street in Penticton.

DRIVING NORTHEAST ON FRONT STREET, you quickly cross Penticton Creek on a small bridge. This is one of the three main creeks that filled Okanagan Lake with deltaic sands and gravels to form Penticton. It is now largely confined to concrete walls within the city to prevent erosion and flooding, but it does maintain a small spawning run of kokanee. These landlocked sockeye salmon enter the creek in September to spawn in the gravels well above the bridge. The salmon fry drift down to Okanagan Lake and live their entire lives there, eating freshwater shrimp and other invertebrates; in their fourth year they return to the creek they were born in, spawn, and die.

Front Street ends at a roundabout; go straight through and up the hill on Vancouver Avenue. If you have time, a walk along the old Kettle Valley Rail Trail is a good scenic diversion; you'll find it at the end of Vancouver Place on the north side of Vancouver Avenue. The trail traverses the tops of magnificent silt bluffs cloaked in sagebrush, then swings inland. From the top of Vancouver Hill, the route to Naramata winds through orchards to the base of Munson Mountain, a small, rocky hill west of the road. This is the core

97

of a volcano that was active about 55 million years ago during the birth of the Okanagan Valley. A short road and trail to the top of the hill provide wonderful views of Penticton and the entire valley.

The road swings east across the benches to the start of Naramata Road (make sure you make the last left turn to the east instead of continuing south on Upper Bench Road). On the hill to the northeast, you can see the wall of fill at the regional landfill, often easily spotted by the cloud of gulls and ravens circling overhead. Occasionally bald or golden eagles join the feeding frenzy at the landfill, so watch for big birds in the flock.

A large propeller on a tower overlooks a sizable apricot orchard on the west side of the road; the former is an air mover or wind machine. This is used on frosty nights in early April, when the tender apricot blossoms might be damaged by the cold air pooling just above the ground. The air mover blows the cold air away, bringing warmer air down from above.

A few hundred metres past the Red Rooster Winery, the road goes through shallow rock cuts that expose banded gneiss of the Shuswap metamorphic group. These are some of the oldest rocks in British Columbia, first laid down about 2 billion years ago as sediments on the continental shelf of North America. They were subsequently deeply buried by a small continent that collided with the west coast of North America about 180 million years ago, melting and recrystallizing in the depths of the earth, then exposed once again when the Okanagan Valley opened up.

Just before Hillside Estate Winery, the Kettle Valley Rail Trail crosses the road, angling up the slope behind the winery. If you fancy a walk along the trail in either direction, there is a small parking lot on the west side of the road at the intersection. Patches

focus › **Kingbirds**

As you drive along Naramata Road from late April through early August, watch for western kingbirds along the power lines. These members of the flycatcher family, with their yellow bellies and black tails, are easy to spot as they perch upright on the wires. The natural habitat of the western kingbird is the open plains and ponderosa pine woodlands of the West, and the birds used to nest exclusively on the wide branches of lone pines or other trees that had gained a foothold in the grasslands. They quickly recognized the power and telephone lines that snaked across the West as a new source of nesting habitat. Look closely at each pole and you'll see a number of their untidy grass nests stuck on to insulators or tucked in behind transformers. Kingbirds aggressively defend their nests and will readily dive on any cat that happens to wander innocently by, chattering loudly to warn all other birds of the approaching danger. Western kingbirds have white outer tail feathers to frame their black tails; the similar eastern kingbird (also common in the Okanagan) has a white belly and a white tip on its black tail. Eastern kingbirds prefer deciduous woodlands for nesting habitat and are common in older orchards; they occasionally nest on power poles but usually make their homes in large trees or shrubs.

of native vegetation can be seen on rocky sites along the road; at Sutherland Road, saskatoon and elderberry bushes dot the hillside.

There are many good views across the lake to Summerland. Trout Creek drains most of the hills and plateaus on that side of the valley, and its delta spreads broadly into the lake. Drainage on the Naramata side of the lake is patterned much differently, with many small creeks spilling down the hillsides instead of one large one. The large bluff just north of Trout Creek is Giant's Head; like Munson Mountain, it is a remnant of the volcanic activity during the birth of the Okanagan Valley. Its long, sloping north side and vertical southern bluffs are typical of what geologists call a *roche moutonnée* (literally "sheep rock"), formed by the scouring action of the big valley glacier as it flowed south for millennia during the Pleistocene Epoch.

You officially enter Naramata at a sharp corner on the road about 9 kilometres from downtown Penticton. About 4 kilometres farther on, you pass Arawana Road, then the heavily treed gully of Arawana Creek. Like many of the small creeks on this side of the valley, Arawana Creek is very seasonal, flowing strongly only in spring and early summer, but that water allows the growth of dense shrubbery and large trees, important habitat to local wildlife. Great horned owls and turkey vultures roost in the high trees, and bears use the gullies to walk unseen back from their nights raiding peach and apple orchards on the bench; raccoons sleep in the big, hollow cottonwoods, and veeries sing their glorious fluted songs, spiralling down the scale.

Just past Arawana Creek you reach the somewhat larger valley of Naramata Creek. A small park on the east side of the road (inventively named Creek Park) is well worth a stop and a short walk along a trail through the shady woodland beside a rocky stream. Here, traffic to Naramata village goes down the hill on Robinson Road; we will continue along North Naramata Road. A half-kilometre farther on, you pass Smethurst Road on the east; this road offers access to the Kettle Valley Rail Trail, now high above you. If you look north here, you can see where the railroad passed through the Little Tunnel at a prominent rock bluff.

At Languedoc Road the route passes over Robinson Creek, then Trust Creek a few hundred metres farther on. Here the orchards and vineyards end, and the road travels through a more natural landscape, with scattered large ponderosa pines on the hillsides and a dense growth of big sagebrush on the benches. A half-kilometre from Trust Creek, a large boulder overlooks the road; its face is patterned with red-ochre pictographs.

The road makes a sharp right turn into a heavily treed gully, then continues north over a cattle guard with the water birches marking Gilser Brook on the west side of the road. At the top of the hill, the brook has been dammed to form a small reservoir surrounded by large trees. This pond is a favourite with local ducks, such as mallards and Barrow's goldeneyes, in spring and summer. Just past the pond, Chute Lake Road angles off to the northeast, and North Naramata Road begins a long, gentle descent towards the lake. Chute Lake Road provides an alternate, but rather bumpy, route to Kelowna in summer, partly on logging roads and partly on the Kettle Valley Rail grade. To the north you can see the fire-scarred forests of Okanagan Mountain, burned in the long, hot summer of 2003. This fire burned about 250 square kilometres of forest and destroyed 239 homes in Kelowna on the north side of the mountain. Fortunately, a hastily constructed firebreak and well-timed back burn halted the fire's southward advance on Naramata.

Chute Creek roars beneath the road, spilling out of a narrow, rocky gorge. Here the hillsides are dotted with antelope brush—this is one of the northernmost outposts of this plant, a characteristic species of dry pine forests and intermontane grasslands throughout the West. At the entrance to Paradise Ranch, the main road turns left down the hill, passing spectacular silt bluffs on its way to the lake. · · · · · · · · · · · · · · · · · ·

CENTRAL OKANAGAN

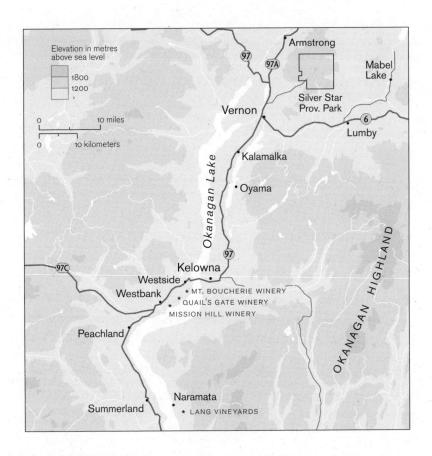

Elevation in metres
above sea level

1800
1200

0 ——— 10 miles
0 ——— 10 kilometers

Armstrong

97

97A

Silver Star
Prov. Park

Mabel
Lake

Vernon

6

Lumby

Kalamalka

Oyama

Okanagan Lake

97

97C

Kelowna

Westside

Westbank

★ MT. BOUCHERIE WINERY
★ QUAIL'S GATE WINERY
MISSION HILL WINERY

OKANAGAN HIGHLAND

Peachland

Naramata

Summerland

★ LANG VINEYARDS

12

SUMMERLAND TO PRINCETON VIA OSPREY LAKE

94 km (36 km gravel, 58 km paved)

This can be taken as a slower, quieter route from Summerland to Princeton if you are headed west or simply the first half of a loop day trip. It is mostly a good gravel road through the Trout Creek valley, then paved from Osprey Lake to Princeton.

START: Intersection of Highway 97 and Rosedale Avenue in Summerland.

FOLLOW ROSEDALE AVENUE south from the highway for about a kilometre; it then turns west and becomes Prairie Valley Road. The road travels through suburban housing for another kilometre, then skirts the lower slopes of a steep, grassy ridge. The ridge is dotted with ponderosa pines, the common pine species at these lower elevations, easily distinguished by its long needles and reddish, jigsaw-puzzle bark. Once around the southern side of the ridge, the road enters the main part of Prairie Valley. This was one of the first parts of Summerland to be settled, since Prairie Creek was a consistent water source amid relatively flat land suitable for orchards. Indeed, when the Canadian Pacific Railway came through in the early 1900s, Prairie Valley was often called "Millionaire's Row" because many wealthy investors bought land here.

The valley is still filled with orchards and vineyards, and large, mature apple trees populate quite a few acres, a rare sight in these days of high-density dwarf-tree plantings and conversions to vineyards. Near the west end of the valley, turn right on Doherty Avenue, then left again to follow the main road. That will bring

105

you to a major T-junction; keep right here, following the small sign indicating the way to Princeton. The road leaves the lush green orchards behind and enters a woodland of young ponderosa pines.

Like much of the Okanagan landscape, the bench you are driving on is an artifact of the last days of the Pleistocene Epoch, when the ice sheets were melting in place and vast quantities of sand, gravel, and rubble flowed into the valleys. Drainage patterns changed dramatically as ice dams melted away. A lobe of the valley glacier extended up Prairie Valley, pushing glacial debris ahead of itself to form distinctive ridges just south of this road. Here, also, sand and gravel was deposited by meltwater streams against the large, stagnant glacier in the valley bottom to form kame terraces. Elsewhere, the roaring meltwaters poured into Glacial Lake Penticton, creating sandy deltas that now lie high above the present level of Okanagan Lake. These sand and gravel deposits are now extensively mined for use in road construction and concrete production.

About 10 kilometres from the highway, the road comes close to Trout Creek for the first time, its course marked by stands of large black cottonwoods. These riparian woodlands are important habitat for many wildlife species, offering water, shade, and food during the hot summer and hollow trees for roosting and nesting throughout the year. Between the road and the creek is the abandoned Kettle Valley Railway grade, now a hiking and biking trail. The railway follows the same route as the road all the way to Princeton.

At the next junction keep going straight (don't turn right), and you'll be on Princeton–Summerland Road. The road climbs out of the Trout Creek valley bottom to emerge on an expansive, south-facing slope covered with bluebunch wheatgrass. The treeless grasslands give this slope its local name: the Bald Range. The first open stretch has a lot of rabbitbrush—low, grey shrubs that glow with yellow flowers in late summer. In spring the grass is spangled with wildflowers—bright yellow balsamroot in May and sky-blue lupines and indigo larkspur in early June. The pavement ends here, but the road continues as a wide, well-maintained gravel road before becoming paved again at Osprey Lake.

Gullies in the hillside are marked by aspen copses and choke-cherry tangles where water is channelled after rainfalls. Other shrubs in these grasslands—the wax currant with its translucent red berries and the saskatoons with their fat, dark purple berries—provide more fruit for bears and birds alike. The currants are also important in early spring—their cream flowers are one of the earli-est blooms in these hills, and the local hummingbirds time their arrival to coincide with the currant blossoms. The saskatoons ripen in early July, and the chokecherries turn a rich black-red in August, feeding flocks of migrant robins, thrushes, tanagers, and other birds.

Watch for mountain bluebirds flitting over the grass. The males are a glowing sky-blue all over, whereas the females are grey but show blue flashes in their wings and tail when they fly. They nest in woodpecker holes in the aspens, as well as in any of the nest boxes scattered along this road. The boxes also provide homes for tree swallows, house wrens, deer mice, chipmunks, and other cavity-nesting species.

The road keeps a steady traverse of the mountainside at about 900 metres elevation. As you get closer to the creek, the road fol-lows a bench densely forested with young lodgepole pine and older ponderosa pines. The sandy forest floor is carpeted with sil-very mats of pussytoes—their grey colour comes from the densely haired leaves, designed to reduce water loss. The road begins a short descent to the creek about 10 kilometres past the end of the pavement; the rocky hillside here is brightened by the pale purple penstemons clustered on the rocks in early summer.

As you near the shady valley bottom along the creek, the forest is quickly dominated by Douglas-fir, and along the creek itself there is a dense growth of spruce, willow, birch, and a few large cottonwoods. Trout Creek may not seem ideal duck habitat, but two species like these mountain streams. Common mergansers are large ducks with narrow red bills designed to catch and hold slippery fish. The females nest in large hollow trees or crevices in streamside cliffs. Harlequin ducks are smaller and feed on the rich fauna of invertebrates that cling to the rocks in creeks such as this. They spend much of the year diving into the surf along the wave-washed rocky shores of the Pacific coast but return to the mountains in spring to nest. The males are blue-grey with dramatic patterns of white, black, and red stripes; the females are more somberly dressed in dark brown with two white face spots. As in other ducks, the female carries out all the nesting chores; the male returns to the coast in early summer after his mating duties are done.

There is a small forest recreation campsite at the creek, and just beyond the road the Kettle Valley Railway crosses the trail once again. As I write this in 2008, the Douglas-fir forests along Trout Creek are being affected by western spruce budworm—many trees have lost significant foliage. The western spruce budworm is somewhat misnamed, since it feeds primarily on the needles of Douglas-fir. The budworm cycle is one of the big natural cycles in the coniferous forests, and budworm populations have been low for the past decade or so but are now on the rise. One bird that has had an impact on the budworms is the evening grosbeak, a big, colourful finch found throughout the coniferous forests of Canada. Evening grosbeaks are named for their hefty beaks, which they use throughout the year to crack open heavy seeds. But in early summer they like to feed spruce budworm caterpillars to their young. From the 1960s through the early 1990s, the three budworm species found in Canada were all at the high end of their population cycle, and grosbeaks boomed in numbers and moved eastward across the country. From 1995 to 2005, their population plummeted along with the budworm population, but this spring the woods are full of grosbeaks once again.

The road crosses Trout Creek again only 2 kilometres on. The valley opens up here, and the creek flows a little less hurriedly through a dense growth of willows. Like many streams in British Columbia, Trout Creek has been impacted by logging activities near its banks, and forest managers and concerned citizen groups have undertaken several habitat restoration projects along this stretch to improve habitat in and near the stream. Logs have been strategically placed in the water to slow peak flows and create pools, and willow shoots have been planted along unvegetated banks to provide shade and reduce erosion. The log structures are simple revetments—a term initially used to describe fortifications that reduced the blast of explosives but now more commonly used for structures designed to absorb the impact of water, whether along a seashore or within a river.

The vegetation along the road shows signs of the cooler temperatures of higher altitude. Mature spruce line the creek, with a dense understory of red-osier dogwood. Red elderberry, a species associated more with coastal forests than woodlands of the dry Interior, appears on the roadside, replacing its dry-woodland, low-elevation cousin, the blue elderberry. But local conditions are variable; when the road traverses a dry, gravelly bench, the forest is a dense growth of young lodgepole pine, the only tree able to germinate in this well-drained soil.

After crossing a cattle guard, you enter land owned by the Trout Creek Ranch. Beyond the ranch buildings, the forest has more mature lodgepole pines; many of these larger pines have been recently killed by mountain pine beetle as that forest insect extends its massive epidemic across the British Columbia Interior. The beetles prefer larger pines, which try to fight back by expelling the beetles in pitch tubes extruded from the bark. But under the constant onslaught that has been underway for the past decade or so, the trees almost always lose. By the time you read this, the majority of the pines along this route, both lodgepole and ponderosa, may well be dead.

The understory of these dry forests is dominated by spreading juniper and the grey-leaved shrub soopolallie, also known as soapberry. Soopolallie was a major source of berries for local indigenous peoples. The berries can be whipped up into a frothy concoction, but they are intensely bitter and definitely an acquired taste. Bears love them as well and will eat thousands of berries each day to put on weight for their winter sleep.

About 40 kilometres from the highway, the road passes the Thirsk Reservoir, the major water source for the Summerland area. The local water supply has been problematic in recent years, and in some dry summers, the lower stretches of the creek essentially dried up because of the demand for domestic and agricultural supply. In 2008 the Thirsk Dam was raised and strengthened to almost double the water supply and allow a more reliable flow of water in the creek during dry summers. About 5 kilometres beyond the reservoir, the road crosses Trout Creek for the last time as it

< black bear

focus › **Bears**

The Bald Range is a good place to see bears in summer—I remember watching one particularly well-fed black bear lying on its back in one of these gullies, raking in the chokecherries with its paws. Black bears are the common bear species in the Okanagan, and local individuals can be any colour, from blonde through brown to jet black. Grizzly bears are much rarer here; only a handful survive on the plateaus surrounding the valley. Grizzlies can be identified by their big shoulder hump, broad, dish-shaped face, and (if you're really close) finger-length claws. Both species are predominantly vegetarian, eating fresh grass and dandelions in spring and roots and berries in summer and fall. If summer weather results in a poor berry crop, large numbers of black bears descend into the valley, attracted by the bounty of peaches, plums, apples, and grapes. Some individuals have peculiar tastes—a grizzly visited Lang Vineyards in Naramata in 1998, digging up irrigation piping and chewing on the crunchy PVC tubes.

comes out of the plateau to the north from its beginnings in Head-water Lakes above Peachland.

You now enter the Hayes Creek watershed, which flows through three lakes in this pass—Osprey, Link, and Chain—and down to the south to empty into the Similkameen River east of Princeton. The three lakes are a popular summer fishing destination and are surrounded by cabins and homes. The road is paved from here to Princeton. The road approaches only one of these lakes, Chain, closely.

While passing Chain Lake, keep an eye out for ospreys, large, fish-eating hawks that build bulky stick nests on top of poles or dead trees. From the 1940s to 1980s, the world osprey population declined drastically from the effects of the pesticide DDT. This chemical interfered with the ability of female birds to produce normal eggshells, so the eggs they laid often broke before hatching. In British Columbia, population decline was compounded by campaigns in the 1940s to shoot ospreys and destroy their nests, because they were considered a pest species that competed for sport fish. When I was growing up in the 1950s and 1960s, the only places that ospreys nested in the Okanagan Valley were plateau lakes such as Osprey Lake. Fortunately, a ban on the use of DDT in the 1970s, combined with a halt to the open persecution of the birds, resulted in a dramatic increase in osprey numbers throughout the Okanagan Valley and the world in general.

The road follows the Hayes Creek valley in its slow descent to the southwest, passing pastures and travelling through diverse forests of black cottonwood, trembling aspen, lodgepole and ponderosa pine, white spruce, water birch, and Douglas-fir. About 22 kilometres past Chain Lake, Hayes Creek begins to enter a canyon, and the road swings up a hill to the west. It emerges to

112

an open grassland dotted with ponderosa pine and aspen copses. As on the Bald Range, chokecherry bushes line gullies where a little more water is available each spring. About 5 kilometres into the grassland, the road passes Separation Lakes, a shallow body of water that is now even shallower as the local water table recedes downward. There are several "Separation" or "Separating" lakes in the British Columbia Interior, so named because they were used by ranchers in the fall to separate their cattle from the herds that roamed the public lands all summer. The lakeshores provide a handy barrier to keep the herd from retreating, as the cowboys and their cutting horses separate their cattle from the rest of the herd.

The barren shores of Separation Lakes are littered with large logs that obviously came from somewhere else. They apparently were cut in a logging operation in nearby Jura many years ago. The logs were hauled to the lake in winter in preparation for shipping on the Kettle Valley Railway, but a sale fell through, and many were left in the lake. They present a curious scene in this treeless landscape but almost surely provide valuable habitat for salamanders and other small aquatic animals.

Separation Lakes is a great place to watch birds—a tremendous variety of ducks and shorebirds use the lake from spring through fall, making it a favourite spot with local naturalists. About 2 kilometres farther on, the road passes a small wetland called Wayne Lake—its marshy shores provide good nesting habitat for American coots and ruddy ducks. The ruddy duck is hard to miss—the males have reddish bodies and white faces with big, sky-blue bills. They display to prospective mates by pumping their heads up and down, creating loud bubbling sounds as air is pushed out of their breast feathers.

Beyond Wayne Lake there is a good view down to the cattle ranches along Allison Creek below the road. You enter ponderosa pine forest once again, then reach the valley bottom and cross Allison Creek. Just west of the creek, a substantial patch of antelope brush grows along the roadside. In May these gangly shrubs are covered in light yellow blossoms; the rest of the year, they are best identified by their long branches covered with short, dark green leaves. Antelope brush is found in dry pine forests from here south to the high plateaus of Mexico; this is one of the only spots it grows in the Similkameen Valley.

The last few kilometres of the route takes you through the rural outskirts of Princeton. The terrain is full of kettles here— big hollows in the landscape formed when blocks of ice melted in a gravel-filled valley at the end of the Pleistocene Epoch. Some are filled with small lakes; others are now used as landfills. Turn right at Old Hedley Road, and you'll soon be at the junction with Highway 5A. A right turn here will take you to Merritt and the Coquihalla Highway; a left turn will put you in Princeton and Highway 3. As you enter the town of Princeton itself, you cross the Tulameen River just above its confluence with the Similkameen River. The name Tulameen comes from *tulmin*, the Native word for red ochre. This colourful clay was dug out along the banks of the river a few kilometres upstream of the bridge and was used in painting pictographs on rocks and facial decorations. Princeton was once called Vermilion Forks because of this valuable trade commodity. At the junction with Highway 3, you can turn west to Manning Park and the coast or east to return to the Okanagan Valley. ·

114

13

PENTICTON TO WESTBANK

43 km, all paved highway

*This is another scenic section of Highway 97, a necessary
route if you are travelling from Penticton to Kelowna.
It provides magnificent views of Okanagan Lake
and has a few hidden surprises.*

START: Okanagan River bridge on Highway 97,
at the north end of Penticton.

———————

HIGHWAY 97 CROSSES the Okanagan River, which was channelized in the 1950s to regulate and expedite high water flows in spring and summer. The first bridge here was located a few hundred metres north—right at the river outlet on the lake—because the whole northwestern quadrant of Penticton was a large marsh complex that the river lazily meandered through. Most of the marsh was drained when the river was channelized; the last remnant was filled in the 1980s to create a gated community, ironically named Redwing Estates after the red-winged blackbirds that had nested in the marsh.

The road travels along the lakeshore all the way to Summerland. Spectacular white bluffs, created in the closing centuries of the Pleistocene epoch about 12,000 years ago, tower above you on the west side. The present site of Okanagan Lake was at that time a huge glacier, flanked on either side by a long lake fed by meltwaters. The lake—Glacial Lake Penticton—was dammed by an ice plug at McIntyre Bluff, north of Oliver.

115

Like all glacial lakes, Lake Penticton was an ethereal sky-blue colour, tinted by the fine silts suspended in its waters. These silts were the glacial flour produced over centuries of glaciers scouring bedrock. Every spring brought a new load of silt into the lake, which slowly settled to cover the bottom with a thick layer of white mud. By the time the glacier had completely melted, the mud was many metres deep, and when the ice plug disappeared, allowing Lake Penticton to drain, the silt deposits were left high and dry as the cliffs you see today. If you look closely, you can see the annual layers, called varves, laid down in the silt deposits.

You can always see a few waterfowl along this stretch of the lake, especially in winter. Watch for flocks of American coots from October through April; these rather comical-looking birds are completely grey and black except for a bright white beak. Although they act like ducks, diving in search of underwater plants, they are actually related to rails and cranes and have lobed toes instead of webbed feet like ducks. Coots are the favourite winter food of bald eagles here, so look for these big raptors perched watchfully in the large trees along the road. If an eagle is actively hunting the area, the coot flocks will bunch up into solid masses, each coot hoping not to get singled out by the eagle.

About 7 kilometres north of Penticton, the highway reaches the delta of Trout Creek. Sandy beaches stretch along sheltered bays of the point, one of them accessible through Sun-Oka Provincial Park. The park also preserves a stand of old cottonwood trees. Their large trunks, many of them partly hollow, provide home sites for many animals. One of the characteristic species in this habitat is the Lewis's woodpecker. These are unusual birds; although they excavate a cavity in a tree for a nest site like good woodpeckers, they forage primarily by either flying around in the air like swallows, catching insects on the wing, or by gobbling berries, fruit, or nuts from nearby shrubs and trees. They look like small crows in their glossy black plumage, set off by a bright pink underside. Another good place to watch for Lewis's woodpeckers is on the grassy hillsides along the highway north of Summerland.

The highway crosses Trout Creek on a small bridge. With its streamside trees removed and its banks diked to prevent flooding, Trout Creek is a rather lifeless version of its old self. Its unshaded waters are often too warm for trout survival, and so much of its flow is diverted for human use that there is usually only a trickle left in late summer. As you round Trout Creek Point and return northwest to the lakeshore, the rocky bluff of Giant's Head dominates the western horizon. This is a volcanic core left over from the fiery birth of the Okanagan Valley about 55 million years ago. Volcanic activity was common throughout the valley as the bedrock on the west side shifted to the west, cracking open the valley along a long fault system.

After a short stretch along the lake, the road climbs a wide gulch up to the main townsite of Summerland. In the early days of the town, this upper settlement was called West Summerland, and the centre of activity was along the lakeshore northeast of the highway. The highway leaves Summerland through a large, rocky gap at the north end of town; these are more volcanic rocks similar to those that make up Giant's Head. The highway continues north, hugging the base of these bluffs (and blasted through them in several places). Golden eagles make their nests in some years under the overhang near the top of one of the bluffs, the adults hunting for the yellow-bellied marmots that sun themselves on

117

focus › **Kokanee**

Kokanee are a type of sockeye salmon, and like their oceangoing cousins, they spend the first year of their lives in a lake, eating plankton. But kokanee stay in the lake for the rest of their lives, returning in their third or fourth year to the place where they were born to spawn and die. Some kokanee in Okanagan Lake spawn along gravelly shores, mostly across the lake from Peachland along the rocky headland of Okanagan Mountain Provincial Park. But most spawn in creeks up and down the valley. In 1966 fisheries biologists introduced mysid shrimp into Okanagan Lake, since they had noticed that mature kokanee in lakes with these large shrimp grew to record sizes. Unfortunately, they didn't realize that the shrimp also compete with young kokanee for small plankton, and they effectively starved the small fish. In the early 1970s, kokanee numbers in Okanagan Lake began to plummet, going from over a million spawners to about ten thousand by 1998. The sportfishery was closed from 1995 to 2005, and a number of other conservation measures were put into place, including operating a shrimp trawler to reduce the mysid population. By 2007 the kokanee spawning population had rebounded to 296,000, and sportfishing has been reopened for short trial periods.

the rocky slopes. A small herd of mountain goats can sometimes be seen on the steep, grassy slopes about a kilometre north of town, where escape terrain is close at hand on the nearby cliffs. These slopes are also important winter range for mule deer; large numbers move off the high plateaus to lower elevations, attracted by the relatively shallow snowpack and abundance of food. One of their favourite food plants here is the red-stemmed ceanothus, a shrub that is particularly common after ground fires.

To the northeast you can see the rounded, rocky slopes of Okanagan Mountain, extending into the lake as Squally Point. On August 16, 2003, a lightning strike above Squally Point started one of the most destructive forest fires in Canadian history. Before it was finally put out in the cooler, damper days of late September, it had forced the evacuation of 45,000 people from their homes, burned 239 houses in Kelowna, and consumed 250 square kilometres of forest. Firestorms such as this one are becoming more common throughout western North America; a half-century of selective logging and aggressive fire suppression has created a forest structure and fuel load perfect for high-intensity fires. Native people throughout the West used to burn sections of their territories each spring and fall to maintain an open character to the forest, especially in dry woodlands such as those dominated by ponderosa pine and Douglas-fir. These fires kept fuel loads low and created ideal habitat for food plants such as arrowleaf balsamroot and bitterroot. Today, forest managers are once again looking at prescribed burns as a way to minimize the risk of midsummer wildfires.

After traversing the hillside well above Okanagan Lake for 14 kilometres, the highway drops to lake level at the south end of Peachland, onto the small delta of Peachland Creek. Loons,

119

mergansers, and gulls often gather at the creek mouth in late summer and fall, since the creek is a major spawning ground for kokanee, the landlocked form of sockeye salmon. The creek itself is well worth a stop; turn left just south of the bridge and park. A lovely trail goes up the narrow valley, shaded by tall cottonwoods and cooled by the creek itself. The trail ends at Hardy Falls, where Peachland Creek pours over a small rocky cliff into the gorge. Watch for American dippers here; these small grey songbirds make their mossy nests in a rock crevice near the falls. You can often see them on creekside stones, bobbing up and down then diving abruptly underwater in search of insect larvae.

Continue along the lakeshore, then travel through the town of Peachland, crossing another major creek, Trepanier, before slowly climbing again. As you leave Peachland, the road climbs more steeply up Drought Hill (named after the Drought family, not a local climatic condition). This slope is a very important winter range for mule deer that live on the plateau west of Peachland. At the top of the hill, you pass two small ponds on the northwest side of the road—watch for painted turtles sunning themselves on logs, if you can see over the cement guardrails. Beyond the ponds is the Gorman Brothers sawmill—one of the major forestry companies in the region—followed by the town of Westbank. · · · · · · ·

14

WESTBANK AND CRYSTAL MOUNTAIN

24 km, all paved

This route takes you around Mount Boucherie and its
cluster of wineries to the shore of Okanagan Lake, then back
up into the high forests of Crystal Mountain Ski Area.

START: Junction of Highway 97 and Boucherie Road in Westside.

BOUCHERIE ROAD CLIMBS a low ridge, surrounded by a mix of pastures and rural housing developments. Mount Boucherie dominates the skyline to the southwest. Although it reaches an elevation of only about 760 metres now, Mount Boucherie was once an impressive volcano as high as any of the Okanagan mountains are today. It was active about 50 million years ago, when faulting opened up the Okanagan Valley. Mount Boucherie is considered a composite volcano, formed by many separate eruptions over a long time period. Early flows cooled to distinctive pale rocks; later flows created the dark dacite cliffs that are conspicuous today. Many of these dacite bluffs show the characteristic columnar formations that are created when lava cools slowly from the surface down. Shortly after Mount Boucherie formed, vast quantities of sediments were deposited around it, burying the base of the mountain in sandstones and conglomerate rocks. Millions of years of water and wind and several glaciations have ground it down to its present size.

Mount Boucherie is named after Isadore Boucherie, an early farmer in the Kelowna area who once owned a ranch at the base of the mountain. You can access hiking trails on the mountain

121

through Eain Lamont Park; the park entrance is off Ogden Road about 2.5 kilometres from the highway.

As Boucherie Road reaches the top of the ridge, you can see Okanagan Mountain to the southwest. Much of the forest on the mountain was burned in the catastrophic fire of August 2003. Patches of ponderosa pines remain at lower elevations, however, and in a decade or two the park will be a picturesque parkland of big pines and bunchgrass meadows.

On the south side of the ridge, vineyards become a common sight, and you begin to pass wineries—Mt. Boucherie Estate, Quails' Gate, and Mission Hill Family Estate. Just past the entrance to Mission Hill, you can look down to the hill to the south and see the lagoon of Green Bay. The lagoon is formed by the wave-borne sediments carried north from the delta of McDougall Creek in southerly storms. Boucherie Road drops down to the delta of the creek. At the junction with Pritchard Road, you can see a prominent bluff of sedimentary rocks—sandstones and conglomerates—on the north side of the road. Just past the bluff the road crosses McDougall Creek and its rich riparian woodland. This creek has nesting pairs of western screech-owls along it—an endangered species that requires mature woodlands of cottonwoods and water birch, which grow only along creeks such as this.

West of the McDougall Creek delta, Boucherie Road ends at Gellatly Road, which comes downhill from the right. Continue along Gellatly Road as it hugs the shoreline of Okanagan Lake; within a kilometre it reaches the delta of Powers Creek. The beach at Powers Creek is a favourite loafing site for gulls during the winter. If you have a pair of binoculars, check them out and see how many species you can see. An adult gull (they take four years to reach maturity, and it is best to leave immatures unidentified if you're just starting out in the birding world) can usually be identified by noting the colour of its legs, bill, and wings. Four kinds are common here: the ring-billed has yellow legs and a black ring around its bill; the California has yellow-green legs and a black-and-red spot on its bill; the herring has pink legs, a red dot on the bill, and black wingtips, and the glaucous-winged looks like a herring gull with grey wingtips.

Gellatly Road comes to a T-junction and turns right. Here you'll find the Gellatly Nut Farm Regional Park. The Gellatly family homesteaded here in the late 1800s and, in the early 1900s, planted the first commercial nut farm in Canada, growing walnuts, hazelnuts, chestnuts, and other varieties.

Just past the nut farm site, the road crosses Powers Creek, with another healthy grove of old cottonwoods. Gellatly Road then climbs up the west side of the Powers Creek valley and passes through apple orchards before reaching Highway 97. Continue over the highway as our route turns into Glenrosa Road. The Gorman Brothers sawmill is to the west as Glenrosa begins climbing through a residential area, coming into scrubby ponderosa pine and Douglas-fir woodlands about 4 kilometres from the highway. Glenrosa Road levels out on a large flat with copses of trembling aspen and cottonwood, then turns sharply right and begins climbing again. Many of the trees in these aspen copses are clones—genetically identical copies of a single individual that pioneered the site many years ago. Aspens grow fast and die young but often reproduce from suckers sent up from the roots of a mature tree. This process forms a steadily enlarging clump of new trees, each an identical twin of the original. You can sometimes

123

focus > **Firestorms**

The fire that raged across Okanagan Mountain in 2003 was what forest ecologists would term a classic high-intensity, stand-destroying fire. Started by a lightning strike on August 16, the fire quickly moved over the hillside, fanned by constant southerly winds. Thick stands of timber, dried through a long, hot summer, were destroyed as the inferno roared through the treetops. When the fire was finally put out by an army of firefighters and cool autumn rains in late September, it had consumed more than 250 square kilometres of forest and 239 homes on the southern edge of Kelowna. Although this was an extreme example, such fires have become more common in the last century, and not just because the climate is warming.

Evidence from tree rings and historical sources suggest that before the late 1800s, many of these dry forests were subjected to frequent, low-intensity fires set by indigenous people. Set in the cool days of autumn or spring, these fires burned low on the forest floor, killing small trees, shrubs, and dry grass but leaving large, live, older trees to create an open, park-like forest. Ponderosa pines and Douglas-firs are well adapted to these cooler fires; their thick bark protects them from ground fire, and the big trees actually benefit from the regular clearing of smaller plants that compete for water. The habitat created by these fires was ideal for the local people—food plants such as balsamroot, bitterroot, and spring beauty were more common; deer and elk grazed on the abundant grass; and villages were protected from more serious fires.

In the late 1800s, this practice of regularly burning the forest was abruptly stopped as the indigenous people were forced onto reserves and their culture was severely disrupted. Small trees and shrubs grew

quickly, turning the open woodlands into thick forests, a pattern exacerbated by the selective logging of large trees and overt fire suppression
in the 1900s. These small trees provide abundant fuel that can easily
carry ground fires into the crowns of the large trees. Compounded by
the climatic change to longer, hotter, drier summers, the scene is now
set for more catastrophic firestorms.

Prescribed burns are being set more frequently by forest managers to alleviate the problem, but in many areas there is simply too much
fuel in the forests to safely do this. Careful removal of lower branches,
small trees, and shrubs must be done mechanically before fire can be
used to complete the job. These projects can be expensive, but they
cost only a fraction of the amount spent on fighting a major forest fire.
Public concerns about air quality during prescribed burns and fears
about runaway fires must also be addressed, but the greater fear of
seeing whole communities razed by wildfire may allow land managers
to reintroduce fire as an important ecological tool, as indigenous fire-
keepers have done for centuries.

see the boundaries of these clones in the fall, when each clone turns colour at a slightly different time, producing a patchwork of green, yellow, and orange copses on the hillsides.

Many of the Douglas-firs on the hillside have large, dense clumps of twigs known as witches' brooms. These are formed when the tree is attacked by a tiny parasite—the dwarf mistletoe. As the mistletoe sends its cells into the sapwood of the tree to steal sugars and other nutrients, it prompts a reaction in the Douglas-fir akin to a cancerous growth, causing the tree to produce this mass of twigs. Another freeloader on the firs is the bright yellow chartreuse lichen. As in all lichens, this combination of a fungus and alga simply uses the tree for support. The lichen gets all the nutrients and water it needs from the winter and spring rainfall.

Thimbleberries are common understory plants here, easily recognized by their large, soft, maple-like leaves. The size and texture of the leaves make them an ideal emergency source of toilet paper. The flowers are white, and the berries resemble large, flat raspberries. They are tasty if picked at the right moment but quickly turn soft. The forest changes quickly over the next few kilometres, with lodgepole pine becoming prominent within the mix of Douglas-fir and ponderosa pine. The lodgepole pines have much shorter needles than the ponderosas, and their ramrod-straight trunks are grey-brown, unlike the glowing orange trunks of the ponderosa pines. Many of them have been recently killed by pine beetles.

Higher still, Engelmann spruce begin to show, identified by their long grey-green branches and flaky bark. You are now in an entirely different ecozone, dominated by the spruce and its close compadre, the subalpine fir. The firs have short, stiff branches and a spire-like shape, designed to shed the heavy snowfalls common in

126

winter at these elevations. A mountain wetland appears on the right, ringed by cattails; listen here on summer mornings for the ringing *witchity-witchity-witchity* of the common yellowthroat. If you're lucky enough to see this little warbler, you'll recognize it immediately by its bright yellow breast and black Lone Ranger mask. Just past the wetland, the road ends at Crystal Mountain Ski Area. · · ·

15

WESTSIDE ROAD

65 km, all paved

This narrow, winding road provides a quiet alternative for
travellers going from Westbank to Vernon (or on to Kamloops);
it avoids the urban desolation and traffic of Kelowna and
features some of the least-known views of the valley.

START: Junction of Highway 97 and Westside Road in Kelowna,
about 1.5 km west of the Okanagan Lake bridge.

WESTSIDE ROAD LEAVES HIGHWAY 97 and descends to Keefe Creek, a
small brook lined by brown-barked water birch and white-barked
aspen trees. Cattails flourish where the flow is sluggish, making
this a rich area for many wildlife species. Above you to the west
are layered lava flows of the Lambly Creek basalts, which were
formed only 760,000 years ago. As the road turns north and
gains a little altitude, you get good views of Kelowna across the
lake. The sprawling ridge on the north end of town is Knox Mountain; to the right of that is the bump of Dilworth Mountain, and
in the background is the dark shoulder of Black Knight Mountain.
All these features are remnants of intense volcanic activity about
55 million years ago, as the Okanagan Valley split open.

Some of these volcanic rocks were used by local Native people
to sharpen their arrowheads; the hard, black rocks provided the
name that the Syilx people gave to the Kelowna area: Nor-kwa-stin.
Early French–Canadian fur traders called it l'Anse-au-sable (Sandy
Cove). The name Kelowna comes from the story of August Gillard,
a pioneer in the area. Local Natives called Gillard Kimach Touche,

128

meaning "brown bear," because of his large, hairy appearance. When an official name was needed for the new townsite, Kimach Touche was suggested, but the word *kelowna*, meaning "grizzly bear," was used instead. Gillard's real name is commemorated in Gillard Creek, one of the main watersheds on the south side of Kelowna.

The road winds north along the hillside; as it turns east, you can see the arching shape of the R.B. Bennett Bridge. This structure, completed in 2008, floats on huge pontoons for much of its length. Behind the bridge the skyline is dominated by Okanagan Mountain, where large, pale, open areas are testament to the firestorm that swept north to Kelowna in August 2003. The fire destroyed 239 homes on the south edge of the city and 250 square kilometres of forest.

As you approach the Bear Creek delta, the road descends to lake level, traversing steep, rocky slopes that have a history of collapsing into the lake. You can see the serious engineering works that are meant to hold the slope in place. On the lake are log booms destined for the Tolko sawmill across the lake in downtown Kelowna. The trees are cut on the plateau to the west, then trucked down to the lake at the delta; several bays in the area are used for log storage.

Much of the Bear Creek delta is part of Bear Creek Provincial Park, a popular beach campground in the summer. Perhaps the most interesting part of the park is on the west side of the road, where Bear Creek (officially called Lambly Creek) flows through a spectacular canyon. A 2.5-kilometre trail circles the canyon and is well worth the walk. This is one of the northernmost places in the world where canyon wrens are regularly found; their cascading whistles echo off the rocks as white-throated swifts streak by. Both these birds are found south to southern Mexico and reach their northern limits in the dry valleys of southern British Columbia. The depths of the canyon, where Douglas maples and cottonwoods thrive in the moist shade, is a world apart from the hot, dry slopes above.

As you round a series of corners about 3 kilometres north of the creek, watch for bighorn sheep on the roadside. About ten sheep moved into this area in 2006, having walked about 20 kilometres south from Shorts Creek. Just north of these corners, the view north up the lake opens into an impressive vista. At places like this, it's interesting to try to imagine what the valley looked like 20,000 years ago, filled with a huge ice sheet flowing south to melt on the plateaus of eastern Washington. The rounded features of the surrounding hills owe their soft contours to that ice.

The forest understory on these steep, open slopes is mainly bluebunch wheatgrass, the classic bunchgrass of the West. Grey rabbitbrush clings to the hillsides, providing a glorious yellow show of blooms in late summer and early fall. Large ponderosa pines dominate the forest in places, easy to recognize with their orange bark and long needles. The other common conifer along this route is the Douglas-fir; both it and the ponderosa pine are well adapted to an ecosystem that experiences ground fires on a regular basis. Their bark is thick, corrugated, and corky, blackening in a quick fire but protecting the cambium beneath from fatal heating. Indeed, ponderosa pines deposit a thick layer of needles beneath the trees; these needles are full of flammable compounds and are very slow to break down. Many ecologists believe that this adaptation encourages ground fires that eliminate smaller trees and shrubs, which would compete with the trees for scarce water supplies.

focus › **Pine Beetles**

The big agent of change spreading through British Columbia as I write this book is pine beetle. In 2008 many patches of newly killed ponderosa pines lie scattered along the Westside Road route. Only time will tell if this is the beginning of a major push into the valley that will eliminate most of the mature ponderosa pines, similar to the devastation caused in the Thompson Valley in 2006. Two species of pine beetles affect ponderosa pines: the notorious mountain pine beetle, which has killed most of the lodgepole pines in the province; and the western pine beetle, which specializes more on the ponderosa pine. Under normal conditions, both species usually kill only small patches of ponderosa pines, leaving the vast majority of the forest healthy. But the unprecedented size of the present outbreak is breaking all the rules, and large areas of climax ponderosa pine forest have been killed northwest of the Okanagan Valley.

Just north of Lake Okanagan Resort, you can see the typical structure of ponderosa pine forests today: large trees with a dense growth of young Douglas-fir beneath. This is a transition forest, where the pioneer species, ponderosa pine, germinates after a catastrophic fire clears away all the trees. The summer climate is too hot and dry to allow Douglas-fir seedlings to survive, but the young pines quickly send down long taproots to maintain an adequate supply of water through the summer. As the pines grow, their shade allows Douglas-firs to germinate underneath. Before we started suppressing all fires, many of these young trees would be eliminated by frequent ground fire, but now they grow thickly, changing the open character of the forest. While the Douglas-firs are relatively small, they increase the chance of catastrophic fire, since they provide a conduit for ground fires to spread into the pine canopy, killing the large pines. But if fire is averted for a century or more, this forest will gradually change to a climax forest of large Douglas-firs with a few old ponderosa pine veterans dotting the landscape.

From the sudden scar of the La Casa development, you can see the delta of Shorts Creek at Fintry below you to the north. Shorts Creek is named after Captain Thomas Shorts, who lived here in the 1880s, making his livelihood by rowing passengers and freight up and down the length of Okanagan Lake. The point was eventually bought by James Dun-Waters, a Scotsman who renamed the point Fintry and developed it into a successful farming enterprise. Much of the delta is now a provincial park, including a trail beside the Shorts Creek canyon to a spectacular waterfall.

In the early part of the 1900s, the Shorts Creek valley was home to about eighty bighorn sheep, but forest ingrowth degraded the grassland habitat to such an extent that only three of these animals were left by the year 2000. A 523-hectare protected area was established in 2003, and in 2004 provincial government biologists brought eighteen new bighorn sheep into Shorts Creek and began a program of habitat enhancement. Several of the sheep moved south to Bear Creek in 2006, and the rugged terrain around Shorts Creek makes it difficult to monitor the number of those that remain.

After the road crosses Shorts Creek, it winds back up to a ridge burned in a forest fire in 1998. Much of the shrubby growth in the burn is red-stemmed ceanothus, a species whose seeds need the heat of a fire to germinate. Ceanothus is an important food source for mule deer. From the open ridge you can look northeast up an arm of Okanagan Lake to Okanagan Landing, now a suburb of Vernon.

The road eventually descends to the broad delta of Whiteman Creek, entering the Okanagan Indian Reserve just before Parker Cove. An even larger delta lies just to the north, where two creeks—Nashwito and Equesis—enter the lake only 1.5 kilometres apart. A rich cattail marsh lies at the south end of this delta, and healthy stands of large cottonwoods mark the areas where the water table lies close to the surface, feeding plant growth in this dry valley. Beyond the creeks you can see large, grassy hillsides on both sides of the lake, maintained by hot summer sun on the south-facing slopes.

As you near the north end of the lake, you cross Neehoot, also known as Newport Creek. The east side of the lake here has a rich fringe of bulrush marsh, home to one of only three colonies of western grebes in British Columbia. These elegant water birds,

133

grey above and white below, with long, slender necks, can be seen on the calm waters for some distance, but are more easily detected by their far-carrying *cree-creeek!* calls.

The open fields at the north end of Okanagan Lake are a good place to look for long-billed curlews in spring, and the small kettle pond on the east side of the road is always alive with ducks as long as it is ice free. Westside Road ends at Highway 97, where you can turn left to go to Kamloops or turn right to travel to Salmon Arm or Vernon. St. Anne Road is only about 500 metres east of the junction (see section 21). · · · · · · · · · · · · · · · ·

Townsend's Warblers breed at high elevations in the Okanagan, but this female was netted in the valley bottom at Vaseux Lake while on migration. Encounters such as this provide valuable data for biologists, including the health, abundance, and origin of migrant songbirds.

Water flow in the Okanagan River is closely regulated by a series of small dams, such as this one at Okanagan Falls.

The yellow-bellied marmot is the common "groundhog" of dry, rocky habitats.

Canyon wrens sing from rocky cliffs
from Naramata south to southern Mexico.

Harlequin ducks breed in fast-moving mountain
streams such as Shingle Creek, near Penticton.

A coyote pup explores the summer grasslands near Osoyoos.

The long, dark ridge of Giant's Head in Summerland (centre)
is an old volcano active about 55 million years ago
when the Okanagan Valley split open.

These pictographs are more than 150 years old but are still clearly visible on a boulder along North Naramata Road.

This prominent bluff, at the junction of Boucherie and
Pritchard roads in west Kelowna, is composed of sandstone and
conglomerate rock deposited around the base of Mount
Boucherie by a major river about 50 million years ago.

Peachland Creek tumbles over Hardy Falls, a popular
walking destination on a hot summer day.

Arrowleaf balsamroots blanket Okanagan
hillsides with bright yellow blooms in April and early May.

Evening grosbeaks are large, colourful finches that
nest in the pine and fir forests of the Okanagan Valley.

Ospreys were once eradicated as a nesting species in the Okanagan as a result of pesticide poisoning and persecution, but their populations rebounded dramatically, and they are now commonly seen fishing everywhere in the valley along lakeshores and rivers.

Ring-billed gulls are easily identified by the
black ring around their yellow bills.

Thimbleberries are one of the commonest understory
shrubs in moister forests; their large, soft leaves make
a good emergency substitute for toilet paper.

House wrens build bulky, stick nests inside
cavities such as woodpecker holes.

Layer Cake Mountain, along Mission Creek east of Kelowna,
has a spectacular structure formed by volcanic activity, but geologists
are still unsure exactly how the layers were created.

The dense cattail marshes of Swan Lake
are home to many water birds.

Logs have been placed along the banks of the west
Kettle River to improve habitat for rainbow trout.

The white trunks of trembling aspens are not only beautiful, they are a favourite nesting site for most woodpecker species in the Okanagan.

Red-tailed hawks are often seen along roadsides in the Okanagan, searching with their excellent eyesight for mice.

16

GLENMORE AND BEAVER LAKE ROAD

29 km, all but 4 km paved

This route combines two back roads that tour the hills north of Kelowna, ending in the subalpine forests high above the valley.

START: Spall Road at Highway 97, Kelowna.

DRIVE NORTH ON SPALL ROAD, continuing past Bernard Avenue and on to Glenmore Road. The Glenmore Valley lies between two volcanic ridges—Knox Mountain on the west and Dilworth Mountain on the east. Like almost all the volcanic structures in the Okanagan, these two mountains were formed about 50 million years ago just after the Okanagan Valley cracked open along the Okanagan fault. In the 1900s the Glenmore Valley was a pastoral area, but it is now being converted into a collection of suburban neighbourhoods as Kelowna rapidly expands in all directions. About 3 kilometres from the highway, Glenmore Road skirts the eastern slopes of the Knox Mountain ridge, the hills covered in an open woodland of ponderosa pine and Douglas-fir.

Eventually you leave the suburban developments behind and enter a more rural landscape. Extensive alfalfa fields lie on the east side of the road, then you crest a hill to see the vast Glenmore Landfill. This landfill was created in the mid-1960s on the site of one of the richest marshes in the Okanagan Valley. When I was a boy in the late 1950s and early 1960s, our family would often visit this marsh to revel in its bird life. We called it Schleppe's Slough, but its official name was Alki Lake. As the official name suggests, this was a large alkaline marsh with no outlet. Its bulrushes were

135

filled with the raucous calls of yellow-headed blackbirds and colonies of eared grebes. Wilson's phalaropes flew over the muddy
shores, and the water was covered in ducks. Today the lake consists
of a few remnant salty puddles along the south end of the landfill,
and plans indicate that these will eventually be filled in as well.
The landfill attracts hundreds of gulls daily; in the summer many
of these are breeding birds from the Grant Island colony at Carrs
Landing (section 18). The deep pond along the roadside often has
interesting ducks, especially during spring and fall migration, but
the real birding attraction at the landfill today is the number of
avocets that nest here.

North of the landfill, Glenmore Road climbs into low hills covered by young ponderosa pines. Small Douglas-firs are common in
the understory, suggesting that this forest will eventually become
dominated by Douglas-firs if fire or some other disturbance does
not intervene. These dense, dry forests are one of the results of fire
suppression but, paradoxically, are a great fire hazard themselves. If
a fire starts in this type of forest on a hot, windy summer day, the
small Douglas-firs will quickly carry it into the pines, possibly creating a firestorm that will spread rapidly and catastrophically. Forest
managers are trying to thin many forests of this kind, especially
around urban interfaces, so that any fires that start will remain on
the ground, spread more slowly, and be easier to extinguish. Indigenous peoples lit fires each autumn in pine forests on a regular cycle
to clear out the understory, producing more food plants in the forest, maintaining good habitat for game animals, and reducing the
chance of dangerous fires around their villages.

The road passes two small alkaline ponds over the next few
kilometres; both attract nesting ducks, coots, and blackbirds, and

their warm waters are home to a diverse insect population. Past the ponds, the road winds through rural acreages then enters the orchards of Lake Country. Keep right at the junction and you will reach Highway 97; cross the highway and continue east on Beaver Lake Road. This road crosses the valley bottom through residential and industrial properties, then begins to climb a grassy hillside to the east. The grasslands here are heavily infested with alien invasive plants, also known as weeds. Cheatgrass, a low annual grass native to Europe, is abundant here, as is mustard. The more shrubby plants, such as rabbitbrush and smooth sumac, are native. In some areas sand dropseed dominates the grass community—this native annual grass can be common in disturbed areas.

Bluebird nest boxes line this road—both western and mountain bluebirds nest in the area. The male western has a purplish-blue body and rust-coloured breast; the mountain male is sky-blue all over. Other birds use the boxes as well. Metallic-blue-and-white tree swallows are common, and house wrens have filled some boxes with small sticks. One of the prettiest birds along the road is the lazuli bunting. The male looks superficially like a bluebird—iridescent blue above with an orange breast—but its white belly, white wing bars, and thicker bill set it apart from the bluebirds. Male buntings sing from saskatoons and other large shrubs while the drab female sits on the nest tucked into thick rosebushes.

About 6 kilometres from the highway, the road drops into a small valley. The grassland disappears abruptly, replaced by willow, birch, and even western redcedar, all species of very moist forests. A couple of kilometres farther on, the road crosses a cattle guard and turns into a well-maintained gravel road. The forest slowly changes to a subalpine forest as you gain altitude, with Engelmann

137

focus > **American Avocet**

Avocets are remarkable shorebirds in many ways. They are striking and conspicuous in contrasting black-and-white plumage, legs like sky-blue stilts, and heads the colour of soft rust. But their truly distinctive feature is a long, up-curved bill. The shape of the bill fits exactly with their feeding technique—they wade through shallow water, sweeping their bills back and forth, searching for invertebrates such as brine shrimp. The recurved shape of the bill allows them to have more bill in the water at any one time, and therefore a better chance at finding a tasty morsel with each sweep. They make their homes on the ground near the shoreline, creating a nest of dried mud that they can build up if water levels should rise.

Avocets are birds of alkaline prairie sloughs and were considered casual breeding birds in British Columbia until 1987, when two pairs nested on Alki Lake. The population grew so that by 1997 nineteen pairs nested there. The number fluctuates from year to year depending on water levels in the local area as well as in the centre of the species' range. The City of Kelowna plans to construct a separate shallow lake outside the landfill to mitigate the eventual loss of Alki Lake from landfill expansion—it will be interesting to see if the complex set of conditions needed to attract the avocets can be recreated in the new setting.

spruce and lodgepole pines appearing a kilometre past the cattle guard. The spruce have long, drooping branches and flaky bark, whereas the pines have ramrod-straight trunks.

If you look closely at the spruce branches, you may notice that some of them have small, cone-like growths at the tips. These structures are galls, the abandoned homes of the Cooley gall aphid, and if you look really closely, you'll see that the scales are actually swollen, dried needles. A female aphid lays her eggs on the soft, new twig, and as the young aphids suck juices from the stem, they exude chemicals that stimulate the growth of the gall, forming a home around them. The young aphids mature into winged adults and fly off to found a new generation of woolly aphids on Douglas-fir trees. This generation produces no galls, but the cycle completes when the progeny of those aphids return to the spruce forests.

A little farther along, you will see the other distinctive tree of these high forests, the subalpine fir. Its spire-like shape helps it shed the deep snows that fall here in winter. You then reach Swalwell Lake (also known as Beaver Lake). · · · · · · · · ·

17

THE KETTLE VALLEY: HIGHWAY 33 TO ROCK CREEK

125 km, all paved

*This quiet secondary highway offers a scenic day trip
out of Kelowna or a quick route to the Kootenays.*

START: The junction of Highways 33 and 97 in Kelowna.

HIGHWAY 33 FIRST travels through the urban and suburban landscapes of Rutland then winds through apple orchards as it climbs
the southwest flank of Mine Hill. The deep valley to the south is
the Mission Creek valley, the largest watershed in the Okanagan.
The road climbs on to the grassy slopes of Black Knight Mountain—in the Kelowna area, native grasslands are confined largely
to the south- and west-facing slopes that experience maximum
heating during summer days. The grasslands of Black Knight
Mountain have, unfortunately, been degraded by serious infestations of knapweed and other invasive plants.

Layer Cake Mountain, a striking rock bluff composed of about
thirty distinct layers of even width, overlooks Mission Creek to the
southwest. If you look more closely, you'll see the rock's columnar structure, which clearly identifies its volcanic origins. Layer
Cake Mountain was formed about 50 million years ago, when the
Okanagan Valley was still young and very active geologically. You
might logically suppose that this mountain was built by a series
of lava flows, but close examination of the structure reveals that
it was all formed at the same time, and the layers must have been
created by complex physical and chemical conditions during the
cooling of the lava. Geologists are still debating this question.

140

Beyond Layer Cake Mountain is the broad ridge of Okanagan Mountain, its forests extensively burned in August and September 2003. Near the top of the ridge, due south, is Myra Canyon along KLO Creek; twelve of the spectacular railway trestles over this canyon were incinerated in the fire, as well, but have since been rebuilt to provide hikers and cyclists continued access along the historic Kettle Valley Rail Trail.

The road continues along the grassy sidehill of Black Knight Mountain, the slopes dotted with junipers and rabbitbrush. The low, grey rabbitbrush shrubs glow with bright yellow flowers in late summer. As you slowly descend towards Mission Creek, the grass gives way to forest, and by the time you cross Belgo Creek, it is quite moist forest, with western redcedars along the creek. Belgo Creek is locally famous as the site of one of the most destructive debris slides in the Okanagan. On June 12, 1990, after a period of heavy rain, runoff channelled by a logging road triggered a slide that brought 23,000 cubic metres (about 2,000 dump-truck loads) of mud, rock, and trees down a steep slope, obliterating a house and claiming one life. The slide site is about 4 kilometres up the valley from the highway.

After crossing Mission Creek itself, the road enters the Joe Rich Valley. Joe Rich Creek was presumably named after one of the earliest settlers in this area, but if so, the settler was likely a squatter who left nothing behind in the way of written history. Above the hay fields of Joe Rich, the highway climbs into forests of western redcedar, birch, and Engelmann spruce. These decidedly wet forests seem out of place in the Okanagan, a region characterized by arid grasslands and open pine woodlands. They occur here because the Pacific airflows moving west across the valley pick up moisture while descending into the valley, only to lose it again as rain and snow as they climb the eastern slopes and cool. Birds typical of coastal forests are common here, including chestnut-backed chickadees, varied thrushes, and winter wrens.

Near the headwaters of Joe Rich Creek, the highway passes the junction of the road to Big White, one of the three main ski areas in the Okanagan Valley. Shortly beyond, you go over the summit at 1,245 metres elevation and begin to follow Clark Creek, part of the Kettle River drainage. Just over the pass, a gravel road leads southwest off the highway, providing access to the McCulloch Reservoir and, if you don't mind a long drive on a good gravel road, an alternate route back to Penticton or even to Okanagan Falls. The McCulloch Reservoir is named after Andrew McCulloch, the engineer who designed the Kettle Valley Railway. This track was built between 1910 and 1916, connecting the Canadian Pacific Railway tracks at Midway to the main line at Hope. Just past the junction, the highway comes close to the old Kettle Valley Railway grade for the first time as it crests the same pass and turns west and south to Penticton.

Here the highway cuts through basalt columns formed by thick lava flows cooling on the surface. These flows are related to the lava that covered the Cariboo and Chilcotin plateaus in relatively recent times, between 2 and 20 million years ago. The forests here are typical of the subalpine plateaus, dominated by the straight, thin trunks of lodgepole pine joined by Engelmann spruce and the soft, green needles of western larch. Over the next 20 kilometres, the highway descends fairly steadily to about 900 metres elevation. At these moderate elevations, summers are warm enough to support ponderosa pines, and the orange trunks and long needles of these pines can be seen among the Douglas-firs and other conifers from here to Rock Creek.

‹ mule deer

focus › **Deer**

The fields and pastures along this highway are favourite grazing grounds for deer, especially in the late evening or early morning. White-tailed deer are common in the valley bottoms, while mule deer are widespread in the forested hills. They are easy to distinguish—white-tails have broad tails that are brown on top and fluffy white below. When disturbed, a white-tailed deer raises its tail as it prances away, waving it like a big, white flag. Mule deer are named for their large ears but are best identified by their narrow, black-tipped tails. When frightened, they bounce away on stiff legs in a manner totally different from white-tails.

Male deer grow antlers each spring; white-tails' antlers have a single main beam with vertical tines coming off it, while those on mule deer grow in a series of Y-shaped divisions. Antlers are made of bone and initially covered by skin and a velvety fur; in late summer the males rub this skin off before sparring during the autumn rut. After the mating season, the antlers fall off and are not replaced until the following spring.

White-tailed deer do well in rural landscapes where pastures are mixed with wooded thickets for cover, and you can sometimes count many dozen along Highway 33 in a single evening. Mule deer winter on south-facing hillsides where snow cover is relatively low.

143

A short diversion to the northeast along the Trapping Creek Forest Service Road leads you to a series of three interpretive trails that showcase the stream restoration efforts begun here in 1997. The Trapping Creek valley was heavily logged in the 1970s, and in many cases trees were cut right to the water line and heavy machinery bulldozed the streambed in ways that are illegal today. The removal of riverside vegetation changed the flow of the creek and raised water temperatures so that it became unsuitable for fish and many other animals. A restoration project placed logs into the stream to recreate the pattern of pools and riffles that would provide cool retreats for fish during warm summer days and planted willows and other shrubs along the banks to provide shade.

The highway crosses Wilkinson Creek just past a rest area, then crosses the West Kettle River. This is the old townsite of Carmi, where gold was discovered in 1897, giving birth not only to this town but to Beaverdell farther down the road.

South of Carmi is a large burn—the Bea Fire burned 666 hectares of forest over a six-day period starting on July 31, 1989. The fire started in a sawmill log pile and quickly spread into the surrounding trees. An interpretive kiosk along the highway by the Beaverdell airstrip provides a fascinating description of the fire, its progress, and the battle to put it out.

The road continues south of Beaverdell through a mixed forest of ponderosa pine, western larch, and Douglas-fir. Dense stands of young lodgepole pine cloak flat gravel benches on the west. About 16 kilometres south of Beaverdell, you can see stream restoration work on the West Kettle River similar to that described above for Trapping Creek. Twenty-six log structures have been placed in the river to slow the flow and create deep pools for fish.

At Westbridge the West Kettle joins the Kettle River and continues flowing south to Rock Creek through a broad valley. Many of the wide river flats are planted in alfalfa, though some of them are weedy, unirrigated grasslands. Kettle River Provincial Park, about 6 kilometres south of Westbridge, provides a nice place to picnic or camp among ponderosa pines.

Large spruce and cottonwoods grow along the river, and campers here are often woken by the raucous hoots of barred owls, which love these big trees for nesting. Barred owls are one of the commonest and most widespread owls in British Columbia, but it wasn't always so. They reached British Columbia in 1945, having spread across the forests of the northern prairie provinces rather rapidly in the early 1900s, perhaps because of a warming climate. They quickly moved through the British Columbia Interior, reaching the south coast in the late 1970s. There the barred owl encountered its close relative, the spotted owl, and its aggressive competition—and in some cases hybridization—with that endangered species has pushed the spotted owl even closer to extirpation in Canada.

Rock Creek was the site of a gold rush in 1859, when miners swarmed to stake placer claims along the creeks. The excitement didn't last long, but the numbers of American miners moving into the area prompted Governor James Douglas of the new colony of British Columbia to order the construction of an all-British trail between Hope and Rock Creek. That trail was built by the Royal Engineers under the supervision of Edgar Dewdney; Highway 3 now follows its route, and you can take this road to return to the Okanagan Valley at Osoyoos. · · · · · · · · · · · · ·

145

NORTH OKANAGAN

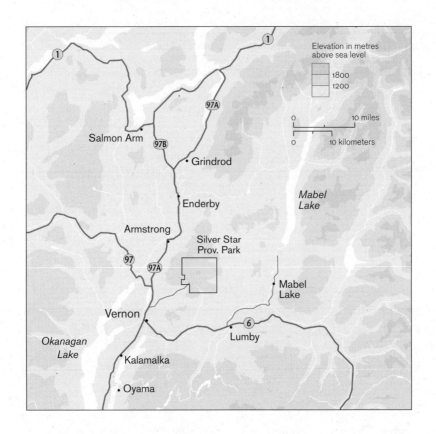

Elevation in metres
above sea level

1800
1200

0   10 miles
0   10 kilometers

① 1

97A

Salmon Arm
97B
• Grindrod

• Enderby

Armstrong

Silver Star
Prov. Park

97
97A

Mabel
Lake

• Mabel
Lake

Vernon

Okanagan
Lake

⑥
• Lumby

• Kalamalka

• Oyama

18

VERNON COMMONAGE AND CARRS LANDING

32 km, mostly paved

*This route winds through the grasslands south of
Vernon past a variety of ponds and small lakes, passing
through the orchards of Carrs Landing and ending at
Highway 97 in downtown Lake Country.*

START: 34th Street and 25th Avenue in south Vernon;
drive south on 34th Street.

AFTER A FEW blocks of suburban backyards, 34th Street turns into
Mission Road, breaking out into the open fields of the Vernon
Army Camp. The camp has been here since 1899 (my grandfather
trained here in World War I), but the structures you see were all
hurriedly built in 1941. As the road continues southwest, you leave
the camp behind, and the slopes to the south are mostly in natural
grass and shrubs. These grasslands are known locally as the Vernon Commonage.

The northwest side of the road is lined with poplar planta-
tions irrigated with water from Vernon's wastewater system. A short
distance from the army camp is the Allan Brooks Nature Centre,
perched high on a hill to the south of the road. This centre (www
.abnc.ca) is open daily from May through Thanksgiving, offering a
virtual tour of the natural landscapes of the north Okanagan. The
building was once a weather station, and that remains a strong
theme in the exhibits about climate change and meteorology. The
Centre is named after Major Allan Brooks, who lived in Okanagan Landing (just below you on Okanagan Lake) from 1897 to

149

1945. Brooks was one of the best-known bird artists in the world at that time and illustrated many of the major books on birds published in North America in the first half of the twentieth century.

You'll notice nest boxes on the fence posts on the side of the road through these grasslands. Local naturalists put these up for bluebirds, but the boxes are also used by other birds, including tree swallows, chickadees, and house wrens. There are two species of bluebirds along this route; the male mountain bluebird is a breathtaking sky-blue colour all over, whereas the male western bluebird is a deeper blue and has a rusty breast. The females are more difficult to separate, but female westerns always have a noticeable orange wash to their breast. The western bluebird is a species of open woodlands, whereas the mountain bluebird prefers grasslands. These birds normally nest in cavities in trees, some made by woodpeckers, others by the natural decay of older trees. Bluebirds began to have a harder time finding nest sites in the 1950s, as older trees were felled and available cavities were often usurped by an aggressive newcomer, the European starling. Trails of bluebird boxes have become a very popular way to help the bluebirds and other hole-nesting species, and the birds' populations have bounced back significantly in the last few decades.

The grasslands here are dotted with snowberry and wild rose shrubs. These provide ideal habitat for the clay-coloured sparrow, a prairie bird that has found a foothold in these Interior grasslands. If you stop at the junction of Benchrow Road (about 3 kilometres from the army camp, where Mission Road becomes Commonage Road) on a summer morning, you'll likely hear the characteristic song of this sparrow—a series of dry, monotonous buzzes. It is certainly not as musical as the nearby meadowlark's, but this song is heard in relatively few places west of the Rockies. The bird looks as indistinguished as its song sounds—as its name suggests, it is a dusty brown above and grey below.

The conifer plants to the northwest are also irrigated with wastewater from Vernon. Although rather unnatural in these grasslands, conifers provide winter cover for roosting owls. The road swings up the hill to the south, angling along a small valley filled with small aspens and hawthorn bushes. Owls find cover in here as well, especially the grassland-hunting long-eared owl.

Just after the road crests the hill, it passes a sizable lake to the west. This is Rose's Pond, worth a stop to check out the abundant duck population (except in the dead of winter, of course, when it is frozen solid). Stands of silver snags attract hooded mergansers and Barrow's goldeneyes, ducks that use tree cavities for nesting.

At the junction with Bailey Road, bear right up the hill; the road traverses a low ridge beneath the earthen berm that surrounds the McKay Wastewater Reservoir. You can soon see this large body of water from its south end. Water that has gone through second-ary treatment in the Vernon sewage system is piped 7 kilometres to this 77-hectare reservoir, where it is dispensed to various irri-gation projects around the commonage. As you can imagine, the water is rich in nutrients and provides good feeding for the many waterfowl that gather here when it is ice free.

The road continues up past the Predator Ridge Golf Resort and on through stands of Douglas-fir mixed with some ponde-rosa pine. It then descends to a large pond, Tompson Lake, that is reminiscent of many prairie potholes, nestled in rolling hills with aspen copses and pine groves.

The aspens are a favourite nest tree of woodpeckers, particu-larly the red-naped sapsucker. This bird drills lines of small holes in the bark of deciduous trees—particularly birch and willow—then

focus ➤ **Swainson's Hawk**

One of the characteristic summer birds of the Vernon grasslands is the Swainson's hawk, an elegant soaring bird easily recognized by the two-toned pattern of its broad wings—the flight feathers that make up the trailing part of the wing are dark grey below, whereas the wing linings in front of them are white. Swainson's hawks also soar with their wings in a noticeable dihedral, raised slightly above the body in a V-shape. These birds eat mice and large insects; in June 1925 local bird artist Major Allan Brooks saw a flock of seventy-five near the Vernon Commonage gorging on a large influx of crickets.

Because insects are so important to the Swainson's hawks' diet, they make a 24,000-kilometre migration in the fall to the grassy Pampas of Argentina. The hawks leave the grasslands of Canada and the western United States and soar down the mountain ranges of Central America. Virtually the entire population crosses the isthmus of Panama, in flocks numbering in the thousands. Naturalists were deeply concerned about the hawks' population recently when hundreds were found dead in Argentinian fields after eating grasshoppers killed by the pesticide monocrotophos. Canadian Wildlife Service biologists and other international experts have helped the Argentinians resolve this serious problem. The birds return to Canada in mid-April; in British Columbia they nest in a few scattered grasslands east of Osoyoos, on the Douglas Lake plateau, and around Vernon.

returns to lap up the sweet sap with its special brush-like tongue. These holes or wells, as they are called, are frequented by other animals looking for a sugary treat, including hummingbirds, squirrels, and various insects. Red-naped sapsuckers prefer aspens for nesting, however, since the trees often have heart rot, making it easy to excavate a deep nest hole once they have drilled through the strong outer wood.

In spring, scan the lake for typical pothole ducks such as Barrow's goldeneye (the males with white crescents on their big, blackish-purple heads) and redheads (the males live up to the species' name but are otherwise grey). As in most duck species, these males will leave the nesting lakes in early summer to gather on larger lakes to moult in bachelor flocks, letting the females raise the young themselves.

You then descend farther down to an even smaller pothole—Cochrane Lake—continuing on down along Anderson Brook, its narrow valley lined with Douglas maple and Douglas-fir. Many of the firs have large witches' brooms caused by infestations of dwarf mistletoe. This tiny, parasitic plant is almost invisible itself, but when it sends its rootlets into a host tree to tap into the sweet sap, it causes the host tree to grow a mass of dense twigs. The mistletoe does not kill the host, but it does slow the growth of the tree considerably. Unlike other mistletoes, dwarf mistletoe does not spread its seeds through tasty berries eaten by birds. Instead, when the seed is mature, the seed capsule bursts from high internal pressure, shooting the sticky seed off at high speed, much like a watermelon seed explodes from between your finger and thumb.

As you regain the pavement on the outskirts of Carrs Landing, the road travels through mature ponderosa pine forests. Look on the lower branches of these trees for a bright green, moss-like

153

growth. This is chartreuse lichen, a fungus that has teamed up with a bright green alga to survive on sunlight and moist air alone. The lichen uses the bare pine branches simply to get up into the light; in this environment it doesn't grow too high on the tree, where it would dry out quickly. Chartreuse lichen is also called wolf lichen, since it contains toxic chemicals that were used to poison wolves in bygone days. Native people extracted a bright yellow dye from the lichen; one of the important uses of this dye was in Chilkat blankets. Interior tribes traded the lichen—found mainly in Interior mountains—to the coastal blanket makers for valuable coastal commodities such as eulachon grease.

Across the lake stands the tiered peak of Terrace Mountain, an ancient volcano that was active during the Eocene Period about 55 million years ago as the Okanagan Valley was opening. Just offshore to the southwest is Grant Island, also known locally as Whiskey Island. This site hosts one of the largest gull colonies in the British Columbia Interior. About three hundred pairs of ring-billed gulls nest on the island, along with smaller numbers of herring gulls, California gulls, and occasional glaucous-winged gulls. The colony was established around 1968, shortly after the large Glenmore Landfill was established in December 1965, only 17 kilometres to the south (section 16). The island was purchased by the North Okanagan Naturalists' Club to protect the colony; at that time the island was renamed in honour of Jim Grant, a well-known local naturalist and mentor.

On the shoreline near the island is Kopje Regional Park, a small lakefront park with a musem known as Gibson Heritage House. The house is a classic example of an orchard homestead built in the early 1900s, when the Okanagan was booming with

154

British immigrants attracted by the ideal climate and gentle beauty of the valley.

About 6 kilometres beyond Kopje Park, Carrs Landing Road meets Okanagan Centre Road. Turn left as the road follows a small gulch filled with wild rose and red-osier dogwood. Okanagan Centre Road then turns into Oceola Road, which descends gradually to meet Highway 97 in downtown Lake Country. You can turn left to return to Vernon or turn right to go south to Kelowna. ·

155

19

SILVER STAR

22 km, all paved

This route goes to one of the most popular ski areas
in the British Columbia Interior and is a pleasant drive
any time of year, providing good views of the north
Okanagan and cool breezes on a hot summer day.

START: Highway 97 and 48th Avenue, Vernon;
proceed east on 48th Avenue.

THE ROAD TO SILVER STAR begins in habitat typical of urban sections of small cities. While some may find the scenery unappealing, a hidden natural gem rests in this landscape of housing, light industry, and fast-food restaurants: a colony of great blue herons. These long-necked, long-legged birds have nested in a grove of cottonwoods for years, flying out to Swan Lake and Okanagan Lake to find fish for their young. About thirty pairs return to the colony in February and March to begin courtship activities; the huge, stick nests are easy to see before the trees leaf out in April. The young leave the nests in late June and July. To get a closer look at the birds, take a side trip north up 20th Street.

At 20th Street, BX Creek flows underneath the road on its way north to Swan Lake. The road climbs to a bench above the creek but will follow the creek valley all the way up the mountain. BX Creek is named after Barnard's Express, the stagecoach company that served much of the British Columbia Interior in the late 1800s. The company's main horse ranch was located in this part of Vernon.

focus ➤ Spruce Grouse

The common grouse of these high-elevation forests is the aptly named spruce grouse. These birds forage on the ground in summer like their relatives, feeding on seeds, berries, and insects. When deep snow blankets the ground, each grouse retreats to its own spruce tree, where it eats spruce needles all winter. Spruce grouse are often called "fool hens," since they allow you to approach very closely, assuming that their cryptic plumage will hide them as you walk by. The males have a unique courtship display in which they flutter noisily down from a branch to the ground; en route they strike their wings together over their heads, making a loud double clap that echoes through the trees.

Once on the bench, the road winds through subdivisions past remnant orchards and small groves of ponderosa pine. The grasslands that once fed the BX horses are now being consumed by sprawling housing developments. At Pleasant Valley Road, 48th Avenue becomes Silver Star Road, and as you swing more on to the southeast facing slope of the mountain, the open grasslands give way to Douglas-fir forests. These woodlands are moist enough to have scattered western redcedar and white birch. Trembling aspens are also common here; their white trunks are smooth in contrast to the papery-barked birches. A little farther on, western larches appear. In summer these trees have bunches of short, soft, green needles, which make them stand out against the dark green firs. The needles turn bright gold in October and fall to the ground, leaving the trees bare all winter.

About 15 kilometres from the highway, the road makes a sharp switchback to the left. You are now entering subalpine forests, here dominated by lodgepole pine and black cottonwood, two species that specialize in early successional environments. These trees are ecological pioneers, settling in areas stripped of their forest cover by fire or logging. After the road turns sharply right and continues to climb, watch for the climax species of this high forest—the tight spires of subalpine fir and the more untidy dark green branches of Engelmann spruce. The firs are easy to spot against the sky in selectively logged areas above the road.

Once at Silver Star Village, make sure you take some time to enjoy the cool air and refreshing fragrance of the forest. The landscape is completely different from the one you left in the valley bottom, and numerous trails lead around and up the mountain. At 1,880 metres elevation, the peak of Silver Star is about 300 metres too low for true alpine tundra, but its open meadows and ski runs provide sunlight for a rich subalpine flower show in early summer. Mule deer are common, and birds typical of the subalpine forest— spruce grouse, fox sparrow, and pine grosbeak, for example—can be seen along the trails. To the east you can see the snowy peaks of the Monashee Range; to the south you can look over Vernon to Kalamalka and Okanagan Lakes. The thick forests of the Monashees stand in direct contrast to the dry, open forests in the Okanagan Valley. These are snow forests, nourished by abundant precipitation throughout much of the year but especially in winter. The record for the heaviest snowfall in Canada is held by the Monashees; 24.47 metres of snow (over 80 feet) fell on Mount Copeland in the very white winter of 1971–72. The Monashees were named by a Scottish prospector who was impressed by the beauty of the range; the name means "peaceful mountain" in Gaelic. · · · · · · · · ·

159

20

MABEL LAKE

59 km, mostly paved

This route takes Highway 6 through the Coldstream Valley to Lumby, then turns north to the moist forests of Mabel Lake.

START: Junction of Highway 97 and Highway 6 in Vernon.

FOLLOW HIGHWAY 6 east through downtown Vernon, with Polson Park on the south. Vernon Creek flows west through the park, carrying water from Kalamalka Lake to Okanagan Lake. Even though this stretch of the route is very urbanized, you can spot wildlife around you. A Swainson's hawk once nested in a big pine on the hill overlooking Polson Place Mall, and a pair of great horned owls took over the site. The hawks have likely moved out of the area as their grassland habitat is swallowed up by suburban developments, but the more adaptable owls are likely still nesting in the neighbourhood. Watch for the hawks perched on power poles as you leave town—they're scanning the remnant patches of grassland for small rodents and large insects. The Swainson's hawk can be recognized by the dark grey hood that covers its head and chest.

About 7 kilometres from Vernon, the highway crosses a set of railway tracks and enters the Coldstream Valley. Just past the tracks, the highway crosses Coldstream Creek, which is flows west from the Lavington area to drain into Kalamalka Lake. The ranch buildings at the railway crossing are those of the Coldstream Ranch, one of the oldest ranches still operating in the area. From 1891 to 1920 the ranch was owned by Lord Aberdeen, who was instrumental in demonstrating the viability of the fruit industry in the Okanagan. Lord Aberdeen also served as the Governor General of Canada from 1893 to 1898.

The Coldstream Valley is a classic example of the effect of sun exposure on plant communities. The steep, south-facing slopes on the north side of the valley are dominated by bunchgrasses at low to moderate elevations, while those facing north on the south side of the valley are cloaked in a thick forest of Douglas-fir. Along the creek itself are stands of mature cottonwoods that require the moist soils provided by the high water table. About 12 kilometres from Vernon, you pass the village of Lavington and begin to hug the north side of the valley. The highway crosses Coldstream Creek for the last time, where the creek flows out of Noble Canyon to the north. This crossing marks the divide between the Okanagan and Shuswap watersheds; from here to Lumby you will follow Duteau Creek. The grassy slopes north of the highway continue, interspersed with open ponderosa pine woodlands. To the southeast you can see a prominent butte named the Camel's Hump, an ancient volcano worn down by the Pleistocene glaciers to its present elevation of just 1,331 metres.

Lumby is a forestry town with a long history of logging and milling. One of the most important local products is wooden poles for power and telephone lines throughout North America. Most of these poles are made from the trunks of western redcedar trees taken from the moist forests east and north of town. Follow the signs for Mabel Lake as you enter Lumby; you'll have to turn north on Park Avenue, then left on Shuswap Avenue, to get onto the Mabel Lake Road. Lumby sits at the confluence of several creeks; they all join with Bessette Creek, which parallels the road north out of town. The road travels through scattered, rural home sites in a forest dominated by Douglas-fir, lodgepole pine, and Engelmann spruce. This forest is decidedly moister than the south-facing slope Highway 6 had traversed into Lumby. About 6 kilometres from downtown Lumby, the road turns east and crosses Bessette Creek, travelling on a broad, high bench. About 4.5 kilometres from the creek crossing, you will see Rawlings Lake Road coming in from the south; birders may want to take a short side trip here. Marsh-ringed Rawlings Lake is alive with a myriad of ducks, eared grebes, black terns, and yellow-headed blackbirds in summer. The lake is only about 2 kilometres off our route, but it lies a couple hundred metres off the road, so you need good binoculars for adequate viewing.

About 2 kilometres from the Rawlings Lake junction, the Mabel Lake Road begins to lose its farm fields and enters a forest of young white birch and western redcedar. It then drops off the bench to cross the Shuswap River just above Shuswap Falls. The original falls were 21 metres high but were turned into a hydroelectric dam in 1929. The dam diverted water through the generator turbines but did not create a reservoir to manage flows. In 1942 another dam was built upstream at Sugar Lake to increase the capacity of the Shuswap Falls generating plant. BC Hydro operates a public recreation site at Shuswap Falls with facilities for picnicking and swimming.

Once across the Shuswap River, keep left to continue to Mabel Lake. The road hugs the eastern side of the valley, going past farms and small ranches and impressive stands of black cottonwoods along the backwaters of the Shuswap River. Watch for wood ducks and other waterfowl in the oxbows. One of the major side channels is that of Ireland Creek, which flows out of the Squaw Valley, then meanders north for a couple of kilometres beside the Shuswap River before joining it. This is an important rearing habitat

focus > **Coho Salmon**

The coho salmon that spawn in the Shuswap River drainage have an interesting genetic history. At the end of the Pleistocene Epoch, the Fraser River was blocked by ice above Hell's Gate, and the Shuswap and Thompson rivers drained to the Pacific via the Columbia River. Coho from the Columbia system recolonized the Thompson and Shuswap rivers at this time, and the Thompson-Shuswap fish remained genetically related to the Columbia fish even after the Thompson began draining through the Fraser River. So today, the coho of the coastal Fraser system, below Hope, are quite different from the Interior coho that spawn above Hell's Gate. The coho populations that once spawned in the Columbia watershed are now extirpated from Canada, so the only representatives of that distinct genetic stock are those from the Thompson, Shuswap, and upper Fraser drainages. These populations are at a very low ebb and have been assessed as endangered.

for coho and chinook salmon; the fish spawn in the river in the fall, and the young fry emerge from the gravel in May. The young coho and some of the young chinook stay in the small channels for a year before maturing to the smolt stage and migrating downstream to the Pacific.

Some of the backwaters have rich cattail marshes loud with the songs of red-winged blackbirds in summer. Alder woodlands line the small channels. About 18 kilometres from Shuswap Falls, you reach the south end of Mabel Lake. The Shuswap River enters the lake here, then leaves it partway up the west side of the 35-kilometre-long lake, at the community of Kingfisher. From there it flows west to Enderby, then north into Shuswap Lake and on to the Pacific. · · · · · · · · · · · · · · · · · ·

21

SWAN LAKE AND OTTER LAKE

24 km, all paved

*This route highlights two rich lakes and the lush farmland
of the north Okanagan Valley between Vernon and Armstrong.*

START: 43rd Avenue at Highway 97, Vernon.

TRAVEL WEST ON 43rd Avenue and drive to the T-junction at Alexis
Park Drive and Old Kamloops Road; turn right here and continue
north. The route skirts wet meadows that are quickly being swallowed by gravel fill and big-box stores, but soon reaches the south
end of Swan Lake.

Large, marshy lakes are rare in southern British Columbia,
where the water always seems to be in a race to get to the Pacific.
Swan Lake is one of those rare exceptions, a lake reminiscent of
the wetlands of the prairies. Set in a landscape of grass and ringed
by lush cattail and bulrush marshes, Swan Lake is alive with ducks,
geese, grebes, and other birds that revel in rich waters. Even loons
still nest in the quieter marshes around the north end, the only
site in the valley bottom where they do so. Swans, on the other
hand, are rare here—perhaps the lake was named after a migrant
flock that once passed through. Most swans visiting the Okanagan
Valley now are winter residents and, since Swan Lake is shallow
enough to be frozen in the dead of winter, those birds shun it.

At the south end of the lake is a small, complex delta where
BX Creek flows into the lake then drains out of it only 250 metres
to the west. A few other brooks feed into the lake off the western
slopes of Silver Star, but BX is the lake's main water source. Swan

165

focus ▸ **Long-billed Curlew**

Long-billed curlews are the largest members of the sandpiper family in North America. They formerly bred throughout the dry grasslands of western North America but now have a more restricted distribution, since many of those grasslands have been converted to agricultural crops. Curlews have adapted to some croplands in British Columbia, however, using large grain fields that are just sprouting when the birds return in late March. In this manner they have actually increased their range in British Columbia, and small numbers breed as far north as McBride and Vanderhoof, in areas that were forested before agriculture arrived. Curlews' loud, ringing cries and long, decurved bills make them easy to identify when in flight, but they can be surprisingly hard to see on the ground. They nest in April, their young have hatched by late May, and by early July all the curlews take flight for their wintering grounds on the marine mudflats of California and Mexico. That is where their long bills come in handy, probing deep worm holes for the tasty occupants.

Lake is now surrounded by houses, campgrounds, and farms, but still retains most of the marsh that provides food and shelter for the birds. It is most populous in spring and fall, when flocks of ducks and grebes gather to feed during their flight between the ponds of the Cariboo or the prairies and wintering grounds on the Pacific coast. On spring and summer evenings, clouds of swallows and swifts wheel over the lake, feasting on the insect bounty emerging from the water.

North of Swan Lake the road meets Highway 97; turn left here (north) and follow the highway for 3 kilometres as it traverses a low ridge. To the north and east are flat, fertile fields planted with grains and other crops. This ideal farmland extends north to Armstrong and beyond; it is the low-elevation divide between the Okanagan (or Columbia) and the Shuswap (or Fraser) watersheds. This northern tip of the Okanagan is called Spallumcheen, a Native word meaning "flat valley." Several species of large birds are attracted to these flat fields—hawks and owls patrol them for mice, and long-billed curlews arrive each spring to nest.

The highway swings west and passes the O'Keefe Ranch, once one of the largest ranches in British Columbia and now a popular historic site. Just past the ranch is St. Anne's Road—turn right here (north). On the west side of the road is a small pond that is well worth a stop if you're interested in birds. Called O'Keefe's Pond for obvious reasons, it often hosts an amazing diversity of ducks, coots, and grebes, and all are close at hand for good viewing. Watch for muskrat as well; these rodents are essentially giant aquatic field mice that feed on the lush marsh vegetation that edges the pond. A kilometre from the pond, turn right on Otter Lake Road. Deep Creek flows south through the valley on its way to the north end of Okanagan Lake only 2 or 3 kilometres south of the O'Keefe Ranch.

167

On the west is Grandview Flat, a raised delta formed when the streams in the area flowed into Glacial Lake Penticton at the end of the Pleistocene. The lake—dammed by ice north of Oliver—was then about 150 metres higher than the present elevation of Okanagan Lake.

Otter Lake is a marshy lake like Swan Lake but less than half the length. The road travels along a ridge on the west side of the lake, so the views are best in the afternoon or evening. The east side of the lake is thickly forested in Douglas-fir and trembling aspen, and the lake itself is ringed with cattails and willows. Near the north end of the lake you meet Grandview Flats Road; turn right and, within a few hundred metres, you'll come to a pull-off overlooking the lake and a sizable marsh. This is well worth a stop almost any day of the year. Teal dabble in the marsh, snipe winnow overhead in spring, and if you're lucky, a bittern might be heard pumping from the cover of the cattails.

Continue north to Wood Avenue; turn east and work your way through Armstrong to Highway 97A. From there you can turn south to return to Vernon. · · · · · · · · · · · · · · · ·

THE END
(OF THE ROAD)

THE OKANAGAN VALLEY has many more roads to travel, all of which showcase its natural beauty and diversity. Some wind along the lakeshores and river valleys, lush with broad-leaved trees; others traverse orchards and vineyards or climb to the cool forests of the mountains and plateaus. Whether you have come to the Okanagan for its sun, sand, birds, or wine, these roads will take you through a rewarding and often inspiring landscape.

As more and more people fall under the spell of this valley, more houses are built, and habitat is inexorably lost. There's a new housing development above my home in Naramata with the motto, "The End of the Road is Just the Beginning." I hope that this book has provided a new beginning of sorts and has given you a new way to look at the Okanagan Valley. It's easy to see the bounty of wines and fresh fruit, and the attraction of a sandy beach on a hot summer day is obvious as well, but the natural beauty of the valley is too often taken for granted.

We share this special valley with many other species; it is small, with limited water supplies and a sensitive ecosystem. It would be very easy to do irrevocable damage to its forests, grasslands, and wetlands through shortsighted development. But with proper long-term planning, there is no reason to believe that we cannot continue to enjoy drives through the natural Okanagan, smelling the scent of the pines on warm summer winds or viewing a valley framed in golden grass.

IMAGE CREDITS

Photos

All photos are by Richard Cannings except as follows:

Robert Cannings: photo section 1, p. 13

Steve Cannings: p. 70; photo section 1, p. 1, top; photo section 1, p. 2, bottom; photo section 1, p. 4; photo section 1, p. 9, top; photo section 1, p. 10; photo section 1, p. 15; photo section 2, p. 2, top; photo section 2, p. 3, top; photo section 2, p. 9, bottom; and photo section 2, p. 13, bottom

Gordon Court: p. 152 and photo section 1, p. 16, top

Alistair Fraser: p. 118

Les Gyug: p. 31

Ralph Hocken: p. 80

Lone Jones: p. 125

Ian Routley: pp. 111, 138, and 166

Illustrations

Donald Gunn: pp. 90 and 163

Canadian Forest Service: p. 131

INDEX

*Italic indicates photograph
or illustration.*

Birch (*continued*)
    white, 158, 163; as wildlife
    habitat, 13, 29, 85; woodlands,
    5, 13, 60, 76; and yellow-
    breasted chats, 49, 66
Birds, 4
Bittern, 168
Bitterroot, 15, 17, 36, 119, 124
Black Knight Mountain, 128, 140–41
Black Sage Road, 19, 42, 59, 64–65
Black widow spiders, 4
Blackbirds: red-winged, 115, 164;
    yellow-headed, 59, 136, 162
Bluebird: moutain, 47, 75, 107,
    137, 150; western, 43, 51,
    65, 75, 76, 137, 150
Boa, rubber, 4, 71
Bobolink, 40, 60
Boucherie Road, 121–22
Bridesville, 32
Brine shrimp, 55, 138
British Columbia Minister of
    Environment, 65
Brooks, Major Allan, 149–50, 152
Budworm, western spruce, 108–09
Bunting, lazuli, 137
Burnell (Sawmill) Lake, 50
Burrowing Owl Estate
    Winery, 62, 64
Buttercup, sagebrush, 14
BX Creek, 157, 165

Cactus, brittle prickly pear, 10, 88
Calona Wines, 19
Camp McKinney, 42
Carmi, 144
Carrs Landing, 136, 149, 153, 155

Cascade Mountains, 1, 14, 40
Cattails, 59, 93, 127, 128, 168
Cattle, 9, 18–19, 30, 62, 93, 113
Cawston, 40–41
Ceanothus, red-stemmed, 119, 133
Cedar, western red, 85, 92,
    137, 141, 158, 161, 162
Chat, yellow-breasted, 49, 66, 76
Chipmunks, 107
Chokecherry, 38, 49, 107, 111, 113
Chukar, 37, 71, 86
Chute Creek, 102
Clark Creek, 142
Climate, 13–16
Coal mines, 57
Coast Mountains, 14
Cochrane Lake, 153
Coldstream Creek, 160–61
Coldstream Ranch, 160
Coots, 15, 136, 167;
    American, 113, 116
Coteay Meadows, 47–48
Cottonwood: black, 106, 112, 158,
    162; along creeks and rivers, 38,
    84, 87, 89, 108, 120, 123, 130,
    133, 145, 161; and endangered
    species, 66; and great blue herons,
    91, 157; and Lewis's woodpeckers,
    116; rarity of mature habitat, 87,
    89; through the seasons, 15; and
    spotted bats, 68; and Vaux's swifts,
    90; as wildlife habitat, 13, 85,
    91, 93, 100, 116, 157
Coyote, 60, 93
Crickets, Jerusalem, 4, 62
Crystal Mountain
    ski area, 121, 127

175

176

177

Mantis, ground, 43; praying, 43
Manuel's Flats, 43
Maple, Douglas, 29, 130, 153
Marmot, yellow-bellied, 82–83, 117
Marron River, 58, 82
Marron Valley, 82
Marshes, 5, 8, 13, 27,
    35, 47, 78, 135, 165
McBride, David, 32
McCulloch Reservoir, 142
McCulloch, Andrew, 142
McDougall Creek, 122
McIntyre Bluff, 6, 8, 42,
    67, 69, 115
McKay Wastewater Reservoir, 151
McKinney Road, 42, 65
McLean Creek, 86–87
Meadowlark, western,
    14, 21, 40, 43, 47, 56
Metalmark, Mormon, 41
Meyers Flat, 51, 54
Mice, 32, 60, 93, 152; deer,
    107; pocket, 4, 62, 64
Mine Hill, 140
Mission CreekFamily
    Estate Winery, 140–41
Mission Hill, 122
Mistletoe, dwarf, 87, 92, 126, 153
Mock orange, 50
Monashee Range, 159
Mount Baldy, 42, 48
Mount Boucherie, 6, 121–22
Mt. Boucherie Estate Winery, 122
Mount Kobau, 29, 34, 36
Mount Mazama, 84
Mount Parker, 82
Mountain goat, 84, 119

Mullein, 46
Munson Mountain, 6, 97, 100
Muskrat, 167
Myra Canyon, 141

Naramata, 2, 97–102, 111, 171
Naramata Creek, 100
Naramata Road, 97–101
Nashwito Creek, 133
Native people (Syilx), 16, 27–28,
    35, 53, 73, 119, 128, 154
Nature Trust of British
    Columbia, 56, 72
Neehoot (Newport) Creek, 133
Nighthawk, common, 74
Nk'Mip, 16, 28, 35
Nutcracker, Clark's, 96
Nuthatch, pygmy, 11

O'Keefe Ranch, 167
O'Keefe's Pond, 167
Okanagan Centre Road, 155
Okanagan Falls: native history of,
    73; routes through, 54, 58, 67,
    72–74, 86–87, 142
Okanagan Falls Provincial Park, 74
Okanagan Lake: Deep Creek flowing
    to, 167; deltas at Penticton, 79,
    97; depth, 8; in glacial times, 106,
    115, 168; and great blue herons,
    157; and kokanee, 97, 118; routes
    along, 119, 121–22, 132–4; Vernon
    Creek flowing to, 160, 167–68;
    views of, 115, 133, 159
Okanagan Mountain, 101, 119,
    122, 129, 141; fire, 101, 119,
    122, 124, 129, 141

Okanagan Mountain
  Provincial Park, 118
Okanagan River: channelization,
  5, 13, 61, 89, 115; Fort Okanogan,
  site of, 40; in glacial times, 7; at
  Okanagan Falls, 73–74; origin
  of name, 16; and Osoyoos Lake,
  formation, 34; at Road 22, 59, 61;
  salmon spawning in, 28, 67, 73;
  Similkameen River, confluence
  with, 38; South Okanagan Land
  Project Canal and, 34, 42; and
  Tugulnuit Lake, formation of, 66
Okanagan Valley: climate, 1, 13–16
Olalla, 84
Oliver: and Brigade Trail, 82; and
  Fairview, 50; and rattlesnakes,
  44; riverside trail at, 68; routes
  through, 34, 41, 42, 48, 49, 51,
  58–59, 65–67, 72, 78
Oregon grape, 86
Osoyoos: and bighorn sheep, 70;
  and Brigade Trail, 82; climate,
  40; and J. C. Haynes, 29, 59;
  landfill, 35; native history, 27–28;
  and origin of name Okanagan,
  16; origin of name Osoyoos, 28;
  and pocket desert, 10, 13–14; and
  rattlesnakes, 44; routes through,
  27, 33, 34, 59, 66, 84, 145
Osoyoos Desert Centre, 35
Osoyoos Indian Band, 29
Osoyoos Lake, 38, 59, 61, 64
Osprey, 65, 112
Osprey Lake, 105, 107, 112
Otter Lake, 165, 168
Otter Lake Road, 167

Owls, 13, 31, 93, 167, 151;
  barn, 40, 61; barred, 47, 145;
  burrowing, 62–63; great
  horned, 95, 100, 160; long-eared,
  40, 151; short-eared, 26;
  western screech, 85, 122

Paradise Ranch, 102
Park Rill, 54
Peach Bluff, 86
Peachland, 118–20
Peachland Creek, 119–20
Penstemon, 108
Penticton: and antelope brush,
  64; and bighorn sheep, 70;
  climate, 40; formation of land at,
  79, 89, 91, 97; native settlement
  at, 17, 89; population growth,
  2; routes through, 34, 41, 49,
  57–58, 66, 72, 78–79, 86–89,
  97, 115; stagecoach route out
  of, 94; views of, 98
Penticton Creek, 79, 97
Phalarope, Wilson's, 55, 136
Phoebe, Say's, 64
Pictographs, 101
Pika, 94–95
Pine, lodgepole: identification,
  94, 126, 139, 142; and mountain
  pine beetle, 110, 131; as pioneer
  species in forest succession, 12;
  47, 158; and subalpine fir, 94
Pine, ponderosa: and antelope brush,
  82, 87, 102, 114; and chartreuse
  lichen, 153–54; ecosystem,
  11–12; and fire, 50–51, 91, 119,
  122, 124, 130, 132, 136;

179

181